BORDER BOSS

Texas Ranger Captain John R. Hughes

BORDER BOSS

Captain John R. Hughes--Texas Ranger

By JACK MARTIN

DRAWINGS BY FRANK ANTHONY STANUSH

STATE HOUSE PRESS
Austin, Texas
1990

Library of Congress Cataloging-in-Publication Data

Martin, Jack, 1901-
    Border boss: Captain John R. Hughes, Texas ranger / by
Jack Martin; introduction by Mike Cox; drawings by Frank
Anthony Stanush.
    p. cm.
    Reprint. Originally published: San Antonio, Tex.: Naylor
Co., 1942.
    Includes biographical references.
    ISBN 0-939349-49-X: $21.95. -- ISBN 0-938349-50-3 (pbk.):
$14.95. -- ISBN 0-938349-51-1 (lim. ed.): $50.00
    1. Hughes, John R. (John Reynolds), 1855-1947. 2. Texas
Rangers Biography. 3. Texas--History 1846-1950. I. Title.
F391.H88M3 1990
976.4'06'092dc20
[B]

                                                    89-48043
                                                    CIP

Manufactured in the United States of America

State House Press
P.O. Box 15247
Austin, Texas 78761

To

THE TEXAS RANGERS

—the old heroes who carried law and order to the frontier, and their gallant successors who as zealously uphold the honor and protect the people of a great state.

INTRODUCTION

Hanging from the corner of an old lawyer-style bookcase in my office is a worn saddle gun scabbard. Aside from the marks of age, the scabbard is scarred from years on the flank of a horse in rough country. The thought is a cliche, but a lot of times I've caught myself wishing that old piece of leather could talk. It would have some stories to tell. The scabbard was given by Texas Ranger Capt. John R. Hughes to my grandfather, L.A. Wilke.

For years, granddad had the Model 94 Winchester that went with that scabbard. He also had a Model 73 Winchester that Hughes had carried as a Ranger. I hunted with the old lever-action as a teenager, but in 1966 granddad decided both of the captain's old rifles should be in a museum and sold them to the Texas Department of Public Safety, the state agency that includes the modern Texas Rangers. Granddad kept the scabbard that had been on the Model 94, however, and I inherited it when he died in 1984.

Granddad became friends with Capt. Hughes in the late 1930s in El Paso, where he was city editor of the El Paso *Herald-Post* and later executive secretary of the Board of City Development,

W.D. Myres shows Capt. John Hughes one of the holsters he had made. Photo by L.A. Wilke.

forerunner of El Paso's Chamber of Commerce. Granddad, no slouch of a storyteller himself, was fascinated listening to Capt. Hughes' tales of his rangering days in the Trans-Pecos and in South Texas. He wrote two articles on Hughes for the true crime magazines, took numerous photographs of the old Ranger and promoted him as one of El Paso's distinctive characters.

My mother tells me Capt. Hughes was often a guest at their home. She remembers as an eight-year-old sitting in the old man's lap, enchanted by his long white beard. Hughes had looked down a gun barrel at many a man, but mother recalls him as "gentle and kind."

Granddad admired the old Ranger and clearly realized he was a gold mine of story material. Years later, by then an old man himself, granddad always liked to talk about his association with Capt. Hughes. I used to ask him a lot of questions, but it never occurred to me, since he had written magazine stories on the captain, why he had not done a book on him.

Fortunately, someone else did. In 1942, Naylor Publishing Co. of San Antonio brought out *Border Boss* by Jack Martin with illustrations by Frank Stanush.

Among other sources listed in Martin's bibliography is one of granddad's detective magazine stories on Capt. Hughes and the memoirs of ex-Ranger Ira Aten. In his copy of *Border Boss*, granddad noted next to the Aten entry that "my secretary typed this for him."

Border Boss, which sold for $2.50, apparently did not stay in print very long. Naylor, a prolific publisher of books on Texas and the Southwest, kept some of its books in print for years, but for some reason never reprinted *Border Boss*. The book has become a scarce Ranger title. Nearly a half-century after its publication, copies of original printings of *Border Boss* with a dustjacket, when they can be found at all, are commanding high prices.

Martin's biography, which has remained the only book-length treatment of Hughes' colorful career, is a highly readable book. It opens with Hughes' adventures as a cattleman but focuses on his Ranger career, which began in 1887 and continued through 1915. During the twenty-eight years that he wore a Ranger badge, Hughes crossed paths with some of the best known figures of the West--outlaws like John Wesley Hardin, Jim Miller and Pancho Villa, legendary lawmen like former sheriff Pat Garrett, the killer of Billy the Kid, and notable fellow Rangers like James B. Gillett and Capt. Bill McDonald. In the estimation of both the good and the bad along the Rio Grande, John R. Hughes was "the border boss."

Joseph Dixon Matlock, reviewing *Border Boss* for the *Southwestern Historical Quarterly* (Vol. 47, 1942, pp. 188-189) correctly tabbed it as a book that could be "put on the popular reading list of all types and ages of readers, as it is biography, adventure, romance, and history enacted upon the large, colorful stage of Texas, written in an aggressive, smooth flow of language packed with western action."

Even though *Border Boss* was written for a general readership, Matlock believed it nevertheless also represented a "serious contribution to

Capt. John Hughes holds the noose used when Jim Miller was lynched in Ada, Oklahoma. Photo by L.A. Wilke.

Texas history and is an excellent supplement to such a book as Dr. Walter Prescott Webb's *The Texas Rangers: A Century of Frontier Defense.*" Since 1942, Ranger books that are a better supplement to Webb's seminal study have been published, but *Border Boss* remains important because its author had Capt. Hughes around to consult as he wrote it. Martin used other sources, including official Ranger reports (such as they were in those days) and newspaper accounts, but it seems the author's primary source was Capt. Hughes himself. The captain was not prone to self-aggrandizement, however, and Martin wrote: "His modesty, however, made my work more difficult."

In the final chapter of *Border Boss*, Martin alludes to a notebook kept by Hughes during his Ranger years. Hughes let him look at it and Martin reprints some poetry that the captain had jotted down in it.

On January 4, 1943, after reading *Border Boss*, University of Texas archivist Winnie Allen wrote Hughes: "I am interested in looking over your diaries with you. . . .I have read Mr. Martin's book and find it very interesting. It is my opinion, however, that you could add a great deal to it in fact as well as interest if you would take the time to check over these events and relate further information concerning them."

Apparently, this letter was Allen's second attempt to get to see Hughes' diaries and other papers. The previous September, Hughes had sent Allen a postcard saying, "I am afraid I don't have many papers that would be of interest to you as I have been on the move all my life and have lost many of my papers." The card was signed, "Very Respectfully/Capt. John R. Hughes/The old Texas Ranger."

Eventually, former state archivist James M. Day succeeded in getting Hughes' diary and some letters from a surviving relative. The papers were placed in the collection of the University of Texas at El Paso.

While much can be learned about Hughes from written records, the captain's biographer did not leave behind a very clear set of tracks. The book's dustjacket offers no clue as to who Martin was. Neither does an advertising/sales piece produced by Naylor. A one-page notice in the June 1942 issue of Naylor's *Epic Century Magazine* calls Martin a "noted magazine author and former New York City feature syndicate writer, who had spent most of the last three years in Texas and the Southwest, headquartering in Austin." An article on Hughes in the Austin *American-Statesman* by staff writer Wick Fowler (Feb. 11, 1943) offered only that Martin was a "former New York City newspaperman and Texan 'by adoption'. . . ." The Library of Congress entry for his book indicates Martin was born in 1901. *Border Boss* apparently was his only book.

Even less is mentioned on the book's dustjacket about the illustrator of the book, Frank Anthony

Stanush. Naylor called him a "Texas artist" and left it at that.

Stanush, a native of San Antonio, began his work as an artist while still in high school. By the mid-1930s he was working as an illustrator for Interstate Theaters in San Antonio, doing ads and posters for the firm. In addition to his art work for the theater chain, he began doing illustrations for *The Cattleman* and *The Texas Sheep and Goat Raiser* magazines. His specialty was western scenes, particularly of men and horses.

This work caught the eye of Joe Naylor, who contacted Stanush and asked if he would be interested in doing artwork for some of the books he would be publishing. During a ten-year period ending about 1942, Stanush illustrated six or eight books for Naylor, including *Border Boss*.

In an interview in late 1989, Stanush said he left art for a successful career as a businessman, but stayed in San Antonio. Stanush recalled that he did the illustrations after being furnished with a copy of the *Border Boss* manuscript. The chapter illustrations were pen and ink work; Stanush prepared the original dustjacket color illustration on celluloid, doing the color separations himself.

Stanush never met the author or the subject of the book he illustrated.

Border Boss, published when Capt. Hughes was 87 years old, was not the first book made possible by the old Ranger's exploits. Studies of Western writer Zane Grey's life are unclear on the actual date, but shortly before Hughes left the Ranger force, Grey came to Texas and spent some time riding with Hughes and the other men of Company D listening to their experiences. The result was one of Grey's better books, *The Lone Star Ranger*, published in 1915. The novel was dedicated to "Captain John Hughes and his Texas Rangers."

Grey went on to become one of the best-selling writers of all times; Hughes spent the rest of his life as a businessman and celebrity.

In the years following his retirement, Hughes alternated his time between El Paso, where he preferred to winter, and Austin. He bought an automobile shortly after leaving the Rangers and used it like a horse, traveling as far as he felt like going and then camping out at night if no hotel was handy. "It doesn't take me long to go a few hundred miles," Hughes said in one of the stories granddad wrote about him. "My friends and I talk about when thirty to fifty miles a day was real traveling." The captain made several trips by car to California, where he visited ex-Ranger Aten, one of his closer friends.

Despite his occasional wanderings, Hughes ran a stock farm near the old community of Ysleta in El Paso County, and rode his horse as grand marshal in El Paso's Sun Carnival parades in 1936 and

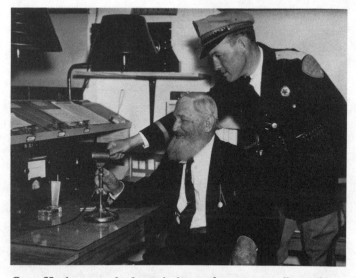

Capt. Hughes sees the latest in law enforcement radio equipment. Courtesy of the Texas Department of Public Safety.

again in 1942. He also was an honored guest at the Texas Centennial celebration in Dallas in 1936, where, at age 81, he served as one of the bodyguards for President Franklin Roosevelt when he visited the State Fair.

Hughes had established his reputation in the saddle, but he was no stranger to the board room, either. In 1929, Hughes purchased a large block of stock in Citizen's Industrial Bank in Austin, an institution then managed by his nephew, Emery Hughes. Later, he served as chairman of the bank's board and was still on the board of the Motor and

Industrial Finance Corporation at the time of his death.

As a bank director, it was clear to Hughes that Texas' cattle industry had changed drastically from the days of his youth, when he helped push long-horns up the trail from Texas to Kansas before he joined the Rangers. "Now days," he told a reporter, "property is fenced in and with labor shortages--all the cowboys have gone off to rodeos--and heavier taxes, it is hard to make much money off ranching."

The changes in agri-business he described, along with his increasing age, evidently caused him to move to Austin when World War II started. When gasoline rationing began, he sold his car, saying he would buy another one when the war was over and start traveling again.

Hughes traveled some, even during the war. In 1944, he visited J. Marvin Hunter in Bandera. Hunter, publisher of *Frontier Times* magazine, knew many of Texas' old frontiersmen and spent most of his long life collecting their stories. Wrote Hunter after the captain's visit: "Despite his ninety years, Captain Hughes is well preserved and quite as active and alert as a man in his sixties."

With the captain when he visited Hunter was his nephew, Emery Hughes, his wife and their three children. Hunter said Hughes "now lives in quiet retirement" with his nephew and family. The children", he wrote, "are devoted to him as a real pal."

In Austin, Hughes like to go to the Texas State Library and browse among the history books, or sit in the Capitol gallery and listen to the proceedings of the Legislature. In fact, during the sessions, he came to the Capitol almost daily. The Senate, in turn, usually recognized his birthdays with resolutions. When Hughes turned ninety-two on Feb. 11, 1947, Col. Homer Garrison, director of the Department of Public Safety, threw a birthday party for him.

Despite the attention he received after the publication of *Border Boss*, Hughes' last few years must have been lonely. All of his former Ranger comrades were gone. The Austin *American-Statesman* pointed out that he was "the oldest living ex-Ranger and the oldest living Ranger captain." He was a man who, in outsmarting his enemies and enjoying good health, had outlasted his own times-- an old horsebacker who lived long enough to hear the news that World War II had been brought to a halt with a terrible new weapon called an atomic bomb.

The captain's weapon of choice remained something he could both understand and hold in his hand--his pearl-handled Colt revolver, the pistol that had seen him safely through his rangering days. He enjoyed sitting on the porch swing of his sister-in-law's house in north Austin, the old Colt in his lap, covered with a sweater.

On Tuesday, June 3, 1947, Capt. Hughes took up his .45, expertly spun the cylinder, and walked out to the garage of his sister-in-law's home at 4215 Avenue H in the Hyde Park section of Austin. Later that day, when it was suppertime, his family began looking for him. They found the Ranger captain in the garage, dead of a single bullet wound in the roof of his mouth, his old Colt near his hand, a rag covering the handle. Investigators contacted Hughes' doctor, who told them the old captain had been in ill health and despondent. Justice of the Peace Mace B. Thurmond ruled the death a suicide.

The death was page-one news in Austin and around the state. A large crowd attended Hughes' funeral, officiated by the Rev. Gus J. Craven, University Presbyterian Church.

As William Cx Hancock put it in an article about the captain in *True West* Magazine (March-April 1961), "The minister's eulogy was inspiring, but two old Rangers, sitting in the extreme rear of the large group of mourners, neatly epitomized the career of a man in whose very shadow the frontier and civilization had crept forward. 'They're burying a big lawman today. Cap'n John never lost a trail. Never lost a fight. Never lost a prisoner. Guess you could say he was *all* Ranger.'"

Capt. Hughes is buried among other Texas heroes in the State Cemetery in Austin.

Mike Cox
Austin, Texas
November 17, 1989

CONTENTS

Todd and the fox hunt . . . A marriage proposal . . .
Four corpses in the Rio Grande . . . Identification by
dental work . . . Conviction of Dick Duncan . . . The
tragic death of Elizabeth Todd . . . Hughes as a silver
mine guard in Old Mexico . . . Trouble with Bass Outlaw . . . Extermination of two murderers.

rett's proposition . . . "Get me Agnew and you can have the man you want" . . . A personalized man-hunt . . . The territorial Governor changes his mind . . . The truth about the death of Pat Garrett . . . Jim Miller, gunman . . . John Wesley Hardin . . . The Miller-Frazer feud . . . John Selman and George Scarborough.

ILLUSTRATION

PREFACE

This is the saga of Captain John R. Hughes, a Texas Ranger from 1887 to 1915, with sketches, comments and reminiscences relating to certain of his contemporaries.

It is not intended as a history of the entire Ranger Force of this period, yet the reader will gain from it, I hope, a clearer picture of the organization, and of what its heroes accomplished in stamping out the murderous criminals along the border frontier, and making that vast area safe for development as an integral part of Texas.

Those who are in position to know call Captain Hughes one of the greatest Ranger commanders of all time. Their judgment seems to be supported by the records, and the reader will therefore find embodied in his deeds the noblest traditions of the old-time peace officers, and particularly, of the men in the force he represented.

In selecting John Hughes as my subject, I was also motivated by the fact that he was longer a Ranger and longer a Ranger Captain than any other man. This, in itself, is no minor distinction. He won honor as a commander in the semi-military Frontier Battalion, and was held over to become, at a much later date, Senior Captain of the Ranger Force which succeeded it in 1901.

If a man is known simply by his deeds and accomplishments, Captain Hughes is one of the most glamorous characters in Texas history. His color was not of the kind to be daubed with flashy strokes; it was of a firmer, more enduring texture, to be spread evenly and more greatly admired in a true light. The swaggering egotists provided the window dressings for the old Ranger Force, while Hughes and the men like him were getting the job done.

There are no stories about flourishes of gunfire from his pistol neatly trimming off the buttons of an outlaw's jacket. But when his score is added up, it is discovered that in his quiet, efficient way, he fought and whipped many of the nation's toughest criminals, outshooting the surest shots even after they were already drawing a bead. The Rio Grande murderers themselves gave him the title of "Border Boss."

Captain Hughes was forced to kill many men to insure the peace and security of the citizens of Texas. For that the state owes him much. It was an unpleasant duty which he performed in the same cool manner that he would have disposed of a deadly rattler on a school picnic-ground, or a blood-thirsty wolf running through a cattleman's herd.

He found duty well done its own reward, and more often than not turned credit for his own accomplishments to his men. They loved him for this, and for his loyalty, his kindnesses, his courage, and for his mental and physical strength which inspired them in moments of danger.

I am deeply grateful for the Captain's unlimited patience in answering my questions, his unfailing courtesy, and his thoughtful cooperation in preparing the material for this book. His inherent sense of modesty kept him from telling me some things, but I learned about them from other sources, and by pinning him down obtained the necessary verification.

These chapters are based on Ranger records and archives, supplemented and enriched by Captain Hughes' reminiscences, and the statements of the old-timers along the border who could tell me of the events which occurred around them.

Many persons were of great assistance while I was gathering the material. The staffs in charge of the Texas Collection at the University of Texas Library, and of the archives at the State Library, were gracious and helpful. John Shuttleworth, friend and associate, was a source of inspiration and great assistance. I am especially appreciative of the kindness of the

Hon. Everett Ewing Townsend, of Alpine, former member of the Texas legislature, one-time Sheriff of Brewster County, a River Guard, and for a short period a private in Captain Hughes' Ranger company. He went to considerable trouble in locating my writing-room in Austin, and in setting me right on many details. Mrs. Townsend was a cousin of Frank Jones, Captain Hughes' predecessor as Company D commander.

"Old residenters" of Rio Grande City, Eagle Pass, Sanderson, Alpine, Marfa, Ysleta and El Paso supplied information I could not have obtained from other sources. Judge W. Van Sickle, of Alpine, who frequently signed warrants served by Hughes and his men, gave freely of his recollections.

To all of these, and to the many others not mentioned, I extend my sincerest thanks.

Approaching his ninetieth year, Judge Van Sickle suffered a fall and was bed-ridden, but his pain did not dull his wit.

"The Indians killed a great many people in Brewster County," he told me. "I recall coming down from Fort Davis in a stagecoach, and being attacked by a couple of hundred braves. There were half a dozen of us whites, including a pretty young schoolma'm.

"Well, we fought as best we could, and tried to out-run them, but it wasn't much use. They came at us from all sides. Then the stage rolled over on a sharp curve, and I decided we were lost."

The judge paused dramatically, and his eyelids flickered.

"Yes sir, that was the end. Those Indians killed us all—every last one of us."

I have saved until the last, payment of my respects to Capt. Roy W. Aldrich, Quartermaster of the Ranger Force at Austin, and an old hero I am proud to call friend. His period of service began in 1915 six weeks after Captain Hughes' ended, and he is second only to the Border Boss in total length of service, and in years of duty as a captain. He may yet set a new record in the first category.

The story of Captain Aldrich's life will make an exciting volume, and one of the noteworthy chapters will deal with a raid he led against a notorious gambling room in the Eastland County oil field. He and three privates cowed nearly a hundred men, and took eighty-seven to court. It was said that when they marched their prisoners out of the hall, the floor was covered knee-deep with six-shooters and automatics, hastily dropped by the gamblers. Obviously this is a slight exaggeration, but it is none-the-less indicative of the achievement.

Captain Aldrich has one of the largest private libraries in Texas—six thousand volumes, including the finest private collection of Texana in existence. Rare books line the high walls of an entire floor of his beautiful ranch home on the outskirts of Austin. He allowed me to browse, and my shadow darkened his door so frequently that he would have been justified in wondering why I did not move in and pay rent.

I shall be forever grateful for his patience and encouragement.

And now I give you the Border Boss, Capt. John R. Hughes—Texas Ranger. If he seems like a hero from fiction, that is the way he was —a real life character whose deeds and adventures were almost too good to be true.

J. M.

March 1, 1942.

CHAPTER I

IT WAS COMMON TALK
around the Choctaw Agency in Indian Territory back in 1870 that surly Art Rivers, the
tall, angular Arkansan who held authority to
trade with the tribe, would some day cuss the
wrong brave and pay dearly for his sharp
words. No matter that the Choctaws had come

under the influence of civilization, they were nevertheless redskins with temperaments the same as their more savage brethren.

Rivers' young assistant thought of this gossip as he listened to his employer berate three Indians one midsummer afternoon. The trader had gone to the Choctaw farm to close a bargain for the dozen hogs wallowing in a mud hole inside the small corral. Much to his consternation, however, the braves were demanding a price far above his quotation.

"So help me, Willie," Rivers thundered— Willie was the name he used indiscriminately for all Choctaws—"you'll either let me have these hogs, or they'll die and rot right here in this stinking old corral!"

The Indians were giving sullen attention to his words. As they grew tense, the young assistant watched with considerable apprehension. This might well be the day the trader would go too far.

Rivers apparently held no such fear. Ignoring the fact that he and his companion were outnumbered, he shouted threats in the strongest language he could summon. Convinced at length that he was only wasting time and words, he threw his arms wide in a gesture of disgust and turned away.

As though his movements were a signal, one of the braves sprang to his rifle, an old muzzle loader, which was leaning against the corral fence. With lightning-like movements, he swung the barrel around and jerked back the hammer.

The young assistant knew that his employer would be shot in the back in another few seconds. With amazing speed and strength, he leaped forward and knocked down the barrel of the weapon.

At that instant, one of the other braves drew a knife and lunged forward. The youth, catching the quick movement from the corner of an eye, turned just in time to seize the Indian's wrist and keep the sharp blade from ripping into his back.

He wrestled with his assailant and they fell to the ground. The Indian with the rifle turned his weapon toward the rolling figures, took snap aim at the young white, and jerked the trigger. The ball tore through the lad's clothing, without even scratching the skin.

Chagrined that his bullet had missed, the brave seized the barrel of his weapon to use the butt as a club. He raised it high and brought it down with all his strength. The white lad threw up his arm to deflect the blow. The weapon shattered the bones in his arm, but he thus saved himself from more critical injuries. Before the Indian could club him again, Rivers rushed in with drawn pistol and the fight was over.

This fifteen-year-old youngster who had saved his employer's life at such great risk to his own was John R. Hughes. This was his first taste of violence in which death hung in the balance. His instinctive effort to prevent bloodshed and save his companion was one of the traits which made him a great peace officer in later years, one of the greatest Texas Ranger commanders in the history of that famous organization.

It was many miles from that small corral back to the Agency, and long before the two whites arrived there, the pain of the injury was almost more than the lad could bear. He was given the best surgical and medical attention available, but his shattered right arm never grew strong again. It was never of much use to him after that. He even had to swing a six-shooter with his left hand, but he overcame the handicap, and many times outlaws argued that he must have been born left-handed.

Hughes came out of this first fight with the most serious wound of his long career. Men were often shot down around him later, but not once during his twenty-eight years as a Ranger did he stop an outlaw's bullet and not once, either, did he open fire with his weapons until lead was flying at him.

He had many thrilling experiences with the Indians before he moved south into Texas, acquired a ranch, and settled down to the business of trapping and breaking mustangs on the open range. Then he fought horse thieves and won such distinction that the Governor drafted him for the Ranger force, and sent him to the frontier along the Mexican border to help tame the wild, desperate characters who had hide-

outs there. It is not too much to say that he
did more than any other single officer in estab-
lishing order and peace in that lawless country,
and in pushing the frontier from the Pecos to
El Paso and beyond.

Murder and banditry was a profession along
the Rio Grande, handed down from father to
son. In the old days of the Spanish rule, there
had been a convict colony above Presidio del
Norte where vicious brigands of all nationalities
were imprisoned and tortured. When Mexico
won her independence, the dungeons were
blasted open and the inmates freed. They fled
into the nearby mountains, intermarried with
the Indians, and their sons were criminals hard
to beat.

But Hughes beat them. He was never whipped in a fight, never lost a prisoner, and rarely
failed to capture or kill the criminal he set after.
He richly deserved the title of Border Boss, and
it is with this prefix that his name is emblazoned
in Texas history.

His period of service, from 1887 to 1915,
bridged the years between the old and the new
in Texas law enforcement. Hughes was always
a horseback Ranger, but he also was an expert
detective. He tamed the old outlaws with his
guns, and captured and convicted their sons by
digging up court-worthy evidence in places
where they were confident they had left none.

He was required to prove his superiority of
brain and brawn, not once but every day, for
when a Ranger commander ceased to out-think

and out-fight his men, as well as the criminals, his usefulness was over. Hughes was a Ranger captain for nearly twenty-two years. And it is significant that upon his retirement he was senior commander—Captain of the captains.

One of his statements has been quoted often: "Good officers and bad bandits died with their boots on. I guess I was lucky."

He must have been lucky—but there was much more to his success than mere chance. What else there was, this account of his career will show.

* * * * * *

John R. Hughes—the R. for Reynolds, honoring a relative or family friend that he never knew—was born on February 11, 1855, in a little farmhouse near the town of Cambridge, in Henry County, Illinois.

His father, a tall, broad-shouldered, quick-witted young pioneer, had a taste for adventure which the boy inherited, along with a sturdy stature and other attributes for frontier living. Thomas Hughes was a leader of men in every community he entered, and there were many of these, for a rapidly increasing family did not deter him from pushing ever westward, seeking fortune in newly opened lands.

A native-born American of parents who came from Wales, Tom Hughes left home early and twice boarded sailing vessels to visit the country of his ancestors. He returned stripped of cash the second time to learn that he was moderately wealthy in farm land along the Miami River, in Ohio, left him by his father who had passed on during his long absence.

He disposed of the property, married Miss Jennie Bond, and took her to Illinois where he farmed a little, but devoted most of his attention to speculating in stock, grain, real estate—anything that he could buy and hope to sell at a profit. Seven children were born to them—John was the fourth of five sons and two daughters.

In 1865 the Hughes family resided in the pleasant little town of Dixon, Illinois, about a hundred miles west of Chicago. John, a boy of ten, stood many times near a bridge across the Rock River there, and silently watched young soldiers drilling with rifles, preparatory to marching away to fight in the War Between the States.

So one of his earliest recollections, then, was of seeing men handling firearms, with death the certain penalty for their awkwardness if they could not master the knack of shooting straighter and faster than the men who would be facing them.

The boy had little opportunity for formal schooling. He attended classes in whatever country school house was available, but most of his learning he acquired from his mother, a gentle woman of English descent, who had been reared in the city of Cincinnati.

The happiest days of his boyhood were spent

in Mound City, Kansas, a small settlement about seventy-five miles southwest of Kansas City. His father sank roots in Mound City, purchasing a hotel and livery stable. There were saddle ponies for the children to ride, and John quickly showed an instinct for handling horses. With the wide Kansas plains to practice on, he was soon as proficient at riding and roping as a rancher's son.

When he was fourteen, a tall, gangling youth grown up beyond his years, his father gave him a pony and saddle for his own. Thus equipped to earn a living riding herd, he sought and found work on one of the small cattle ranches in the neighborhood. Then he cast aside home ties and rode away with an itinerant cowhand toward the open ranges to the south. It was not unusual, in the times and the locality, for young men to strike out on their own at fourteen or fifteen, and if he neglected to obtain the consent of his parents it was only because he deemed himself capable of making his own decisions.

The youths rode together the eighty miles to Indian Territory, and presently Hughes was hired by Art Rivers, the mouthy Arkansan. To any youngster, and especially one reared in a farming community, the life of a trader was romantic beyond all imagination. Young Hughes thrived on adventures, and vowed that he would fit himself as quickly as possible to trade in his own right—preferably with one of the less civilized tribes which hunted the wandering buffalo herds.

A short time prior to the fight at the corral, the young assistant's diligence and aptitude had so impressed Rivers that he had sent him to attend to important business matters in the town of Coffeyville, just across the Kansas border. When he had completed his calls, the boy rode up to the hotel, gave crisp orders for the feeding and care of his mount, and strode into the dining room with the aplomb of a cavalier. But when he slid into a chair at the long table and glanced around him, there sitting directly opposite, was his Uncle Parker from Mound City.

The tall plainsman had noticed his nephew's boyish swagger and stern countenance. He might have greeted the lad affectionately, solicitously, but with rare wisdom he merely nodded and continued giving full attention to his meal. Of such trivial things is character made. Young Hughes learned the lesson well. Never again did he try to act important, for he realized there might be someone nearby who could stick a pin into the bubble.

Uncle Parker warmed up later, and shared a room with his nephew that night. They chatted about affairs at home, and when John rode south again the next morning, he left promising to keep his family informed of his whereabouts.

He did and later, while waiting for his shattered arm to mend, received a letter from his mother urging him to visit her. He was of little immediate service to his employer, and made the trip. He had accumulated about $100 and spent it all, returning in about six weeks practically penniless. He visited Mound City again about a year later, and this time had to borrow funds to get back to the Agency. This gave him something to think about. He decided he could never get ahead if he kept spending all of his savings running home, so he didn't return to Mound City again for thirty-seven years.

In his later years Captain Hughes frequently commented about this. "Mind you, I don't claim that's the secret of success for everybody," he would say, "but I thought it was a pretty good idea at the time."

The adventure-seeking boy arrived in Indian Territory in 1870, and lived with the Choctaws and Osages for four years. While returning from a buffalo hunt with a small party of Osage braves, he paused to chat with freighters hauling goods across the plains in a train of covered wagons and heard the first news of the great Chicago fire.

While sleeping soundly one night in the wigwam of his friend, a young Osage chief named Run After Man who was a relative of Chief Big Hill Joe, he was awakened by whoops and yells, and the sounds of scurrying feet. Grabbing his rifle, he ran outside and learned that a party of Cheyenne braves had raided the camp and was endeavoring to drive off the ponies, the trader's included. Bullets flew and also arrows. Hughes was in the thick of the fight. The Cheyennes were quickly routed and the stock saved. The tribe moved the next day, leaving only graves to mark the scene of the brief battle.

The only settlements in the territory during this period were around the scattered army forts. Hughes often rode along the banks of the Arkansas River, his pony loping over the sloping hills which later were to be criss-crossed by the streets and boulevards of the great oil capital of Tulsa. He must have gazed across the plain many times, and seen only sprinting antelope and grazing buffalo, at the spot where now stand the government buildings and oil derricks of Oklahoma City.

United States troops kept peace between the Indian tribes, and with their sabers dispensed a certain kind of justice among the whites. But murders, rape and robberies were common occurrences. While Hughes held the confidence of the tribesmen, and was never in danger at their hands, others were not as fortunate. The young trader frequently saw scenes of carnage. Once he arrived at a small water-hole on the plain an hour after a roving band of braves had brutally slaughtered eight white travelers there, simply to loot their wagons.

As was to be the case later on the Texas frontier, Hughes was on hand to see a resemblance to law and order come to Indian Territory. He was there in the spring of 1875 when Judge Isaac C. Parker was appointed to the federal court bench at Fort Smith, Arkansas, and witnessed the beginning of Parker's efforts to round up the bad-men of all colors who infested the lawless district.

He was present in the courtroom one day when the judge sentenced an outlaw to hang, but this was not an uncommon experience at the time for eighty-eight criminals died on the gallows under sentence pronounced by the famous jurist. During the same period, sixty-five Deputy U. S. Marshals from his court were killed in the line of duty.

If Judge Parker did not succeed in making residents of the territory respect the law, they at least respected and feared him. Hughes chuckled with his friends over a story told about the judge in connection with a young horse thief brought before him for sentence. Judge Parker gave the youth a tongue lashing. "I fine you $200 and costs," he finished.

The thief's face brightened. He thought he was escaping with only a fine. He jerked a big roll of bills from his pocket, and began peeling off twenties. "Here you are," he said.

Parker frowned. "And twenty years in prison," he continued. "See if you can pull that out of your pocket."

Hughes moved to the Comanche Nation, in the southwestern corner of the territory, in 1874 and traded in the vicinity of Fort Sill. On the trip south from the Osage country, he rode through the Kiowa Nation and met Kicking Bird, the famous ruler of that tribe. At Fort Sill he became well acquainted with Quanah, the chief of Comanches.

Quanah was a familiar figure around the
army post, and no one there attached special
importance to the fact that his mother had been
a white woman. The young trader heard about
it, and quickly forgot. It was of much more
interest that Quanah was the spokesman for
his people in their efforts to limit the activities
of the white buffalo hunters who were threatening the Indians' livelihood with their rapid des-
truction of the great herds.

Buffalo hunting had become big business on
the western plains. An estimated 1,500 crack
marksmen were hunting in Kansas, and the
clumsy beasts were being bagged by the thou-
sands every day. An idea of the size of the
slaughter is had from the shooting record of one
hunter, a plainsman named Brick Bond. He
killed 6,183 animals in a sixty-day period.

At the request of Quanah and other Indian
leaders, the federal government had set up certain regulations for the professional hunters,
the chief one of which was a ruling that they
must not kill in the Indian land south of the
Canadian River. But there seemed no power
that would keep the eager riflemen within their
prescribed boundaries, and there were angry
mutterings in the tribal councils.

The traders, the settlers, and most of the
army officers at Fort Sill sympathized with the
redmen. John Hughes did because he traded for
buffalo hides with the Comanches, and knew
how rapidly the supply was diminishing. Once
a month he drove out from Fort Sill with a

wagon load of red blankets, and a few bolts of
calico, and joined a tribe perhaps eighty or a
hundred miles away. It was a token of respect
that he was allowed to live and trade in the
chief's wigwam, a tent made of skins from
which the hair had been removed.

Dollars were not mentioned in the transac-
tions, but for purposes of his own calculations
the red blankets were given a value of $9 each,
and the buffalo skins of average good quality
$3 each. Three hides for one red blanket! Calico
was valued at three yards for a dollar—nine
yards for an average good robe. The white man
got the best of the deal, but the braves were
satisfied. Hunting the animals was sport to
them. The squaws skinned the beasts, and tan-
ned the robes.

The tribes usually consisted of about three
hundred men, women and children. Buffalo
were everywhere, and camps were pitched at
whatever spot the deer and antelope were most
plentiful. This game was an important part of
the diet, but the most popular food was buffalo
tongue. Hughes learned to relish it as prepared
by the squaws, and frequently traded for the
tongues as well as the hides, since there was a
demand for them among whites throughout
the plains country.

Never while he was with the tribes did all
the braves put on war paint and ride out to
battle, but sometimes groups of the younger
men slipped away at night, a few not to return.
Hughes was given a message to deliver to

Quanah on one of his trips from Fort Sill. He rode miles out of his way but could not locate the chief, and he also discovered that a considerable number of Comanche braves were likewise absent from their wigwams. When he returned to Fort Sill he learned that there had been a "little trouble" between the tribesmen and a party of buffalo hunters, but he quickly forgot the incident.

Years later he was presented with a book which proved most enlightening. His old friend Quanah, he discovered, was called Quanah Parker, and was described as a character of prime importance in the history of the Southwest. Hughes was enchanted by an analysis of the chief's personal history in its relationship to affairs of national interest. Men who are close at hand when history is made, he realized, seldom recognize at the time the momentous importance of the simple characters and actions around them.

Quanah's white mother, Cynthia Ann Parker, had been captured by Comanches in 1836, during a raid upon Fort Parker, Hughes discovered, and had been raised by the tribe, learning Indian customs and language. Her husband, Quanah's father, was the famous Chief Peta Nocona, who was killed in 1860 in hand to hand conflict with Texas Ranger Captain L. S. "Sul" Ross, who later was an outstanding Governor of his state. A private with Captain Ross leveled his rifle at a slender figure dressed in brave's clothing riding beside the chief. He held his fire when he heard a woman's voice speaking in English. It was Cynthia Ann Parker. She died, perhaps of a broken heart, soon after her "rescue."

And on that June day in 1874 when he had searched so diligently for Quanah to deliver a message, Hughes learned, the chief was leading the raid against Adobe Walls, which was to take its place in history as the last real uprising of the Kiowas, Comanches, Cheyennes and Arapahoes. As he read about it, he could recall the names of several braves he had found absent from their wigwams that day and who, therefore, must have figured in the battle.

Adobe Walls was a buffalo hunting outpost set up in the Texas Panhandle by Dodge City hide dealers. Many years after his retirement from the Rangers, Hughes made a special trip to the Panhandle to view the ruins and gather the full details of the historical fight.

On that fateful June 27, 1874, there were twenty-eight whites behind the stockade which consisted of double rows of heavy stakes driven into the ground a foot apart with dirt poured between. The wife of a restaurant proprietor was the only woman present, and she was ably protected by such expert marksmen as Bat Masterson and Billy Dixon.

On the preceding night, one Mike Welch had been sleeping in Hanrahan's saloon. After midnight he was awakened by the cracking of the cottonwood ridgepole, which had snapped under the heavy load of the dirt roof. He summoned Hanrahan and some others, and it was nearly daybreak before they had repaired the damage. Thus it was that they were up and about at dawn to see Indians charging down upon them from the surrounding brush.

The two Sheidler brothers and a Mexican bullwhacker sleeping outside in wagons were pounced upon and speedily killed. The same fate likely would have befallen all the others had not the men been moving about. They sprang to their buffalo guns, and made each shot account for a pony or a redskin.

The braves had not expected this. They raced back to the shelter of the brush, where Quanah held a brief council, and then signalled to a bugler he had brought along. There was a weird blast of the instrument, and again the Indians charged. Again the buffalo guns halted them.

According to the estimates of the survivors, there were approximately 700 braves in the attacking force, armed with rifles, lances, and bows and arrows. Some carried shields made from buffalo hides, and all were streaked with war paint. The battle lasted all day, but the braves could not break through the stockade. Finally they departed, in small groups, and rode away to rejoin their tribes. Of the twenty-eight whites, only three were killed. The Indian toll was enormous.

Captain Hughes also enjoyed reading about Jack Stilwell, "Comanche Jack," acknowledged one of the best Indian scouts ever attached to a troop of United States cavalry. Jack was his good friend and close associate.

The young trader was in a settler's store at Fort Sill one afternoon when Stilwell announced the sickening news of the Custer massacre.

A woman pressed forward. "The officers—were they all—" she faltered.

"All killed, ma'am—every last one of them," Stilwell replied.

The woman fainted. She was the wife of one of Custer's young lieutenants.

Hughes remembered another incident in which Stilwell figured. A bad Indian stole a mule from Fort Sill one day, and the scout was ordered to effect its return. He was away from the post for several days, and returned empty handed to report to Col. R. S. MacKenzie, the illustrious Indian fighter known to the braves as "Old Bad Hand," due to an unfortunate injury which had crippled one hand.

"That mule must have died, Colonel," he said. "But you don't need to worry about the Indian—he won't do any more stealing."

Later Hughes and a youth named Dan McCarty, returning from a trip to one of the camps, cut the trail of an Indian and a mule. Curious, they followed the tracks for several miles, closed in, and recognized the stolen animal. The Indian attacked them and was killed. Comanche Jack was made the butt of many jokes when they appeared at Fort Sill leading the animal, but he took them all in good humor.

Captain Hughes lost touch with this old

friend when he left Indian Territory. Stilwell, who had been raised by a Comanche tribe, finally became U. S. Marshal at Fort Reno, Oklahoma. He served with honor, then fell into misfortune, and died a retainer of Buffalo Bill on the circus star's big ranch.

CHAPTER II

JOHN HUGHES LIVED
with the Indians six years. He learned most of
their customs, much of their tracking lore, and
some of their language. Then he saw an open-
ing with better opportunity, in the employ of a
syndicate which held a government contract to
supply beef to the tribes. The buffalo herds, so
ruthlessly slaughtered by the white hunters,

were rapidly becoming extinct and the Great White Father, at Washington, found it necessary to feed his wards.

The syndicate lost the contract in a few months, and had on hand about 2,000 steers, most of them originally from the great King ranch. Hughes was hired to help drive the herd up the cattle trail to the West Kansas plains.

No one but a westerner who has seen wild, frightened cattle on the loose can understand the courage required of the men whose job it is to bring them under control. And on the old cattle trails there was always the added danger of attack by outlaws. Bad men of both races lurked in the hills, ready to ride down to kill and rob.

Hughes rode his pony to the front of the stampeding herd one day and successfully turned the leaders. Had his mount faltered for an instant, he might have been trampled to death by hundreds of churning hoofs. On another day he lined up with his companions to fight a group of raiding outlaws, but the approaching horsemen were only seeking recruits for the notorious Lincoln County War, in New Mexico. Two of his companions, Jim French and John Middleton, signed up at double the pay they were drawing, and later figured in several of the gun-fights which marked the bitter feud.

He helped take the herd through Dodge City when that town was one of the toughest settlements in the West. The steers finally delivered, he turned his pony south again, and in due time arrived in Austin, where he visited a younger brother, Emery H. Hughes, who was engaged in the printing business. Uncertain as to his future plans, he signed to make another trip up the cattle trail, this time as a driver with Major Drumm and a large herd of Cross-P steers. He assisted in uneventful crossings of the Red River and the several other wide streams to the north, traveling over the famous old Chisholm Trail, the route across Indian Territory laid out by Jesse Chisholm, a freighter.

When he returned to Texas this time, he acquired a small seventy-six acre ranch near the little settlement of Liberty Hill, in Travis County about thirty miles north of Austin. The land was adjacent to open range where free grass was available and herds of wild mustangs roamed. With his brother as a silent partner he went into the horse business, and devised a program which netted a fine return.

Many of the mustangs bore brands of exranchers who had turned them loose upon moving to other localities. He identified the range horses and their off-spring, and then visited the owners, who invariably wished to claim the stock but had neither the time nor equipment themselves to recapture and break them. Hughes traded, giving a couple of trained animals for perhaps half a dozen or more wild ones.

His range herd grew rapidly, and to turn the deals into cash he had but to break the mustangs for sale. There was plenty of excitement, as

well as profit, for every day was a "rodeo day."
He tamed hundreds of bucking broncs, and
could not recall that he ever met a beast he could
not master.

He put salt troughs on the range to keep the
wild animals near at hand, and also put a good
supply in his corral trap. Frequently he surprised
mustangs inside the trap, and had only to close
the gates. On other days he captured the horses
with an old mule, the mere mention of which,
without explanation, would raise fur on the
neck of any real lover of horseflesh.

The young rancher knew that the range
horses would be out of condition and unable to
run much when he caught them eating tender
green grass down close to the roots. It was then
that he would bring out the mule, and the slow-
footed old animal would plod along while the
mustangs sprinted. At the end of a half day or
a day, a well-conditioned, grain-fed pony could
run circles around the tired critters, and it was
a simple matter to chase them into the trap.

Hughes frequently thought of enlarging his
land holdings, and made plans for purchasing
a cattle ranch. It did not occur to him that he
would ever abandon his present mode of living.
He made friends rapidly, and as an indication
of his position in the community, there was
talk among his neighbors of putting him up for
public office.

He subscribed to an Austin newspaper, and
read in it the sensational story of the death of
Billy the Kid, embellished with a thrilling ac-

count of the exploits of this remarkable young bandit who came from a New York City tenement to blaze a notorious reputation for himself along the frontier. Sheriff Pat Garrett was an old buffalo hunter from the Indian country; so Hughes was especially interested in the account of how he had doggedly trailed the Kid, and had gotten his weapons into action first when they finally met.

No one could have told John Hughes that within a few years he was to be a friend and associate of the quick-shooting Garrett, and of Jim Gillett, the fearless young marshal who was keeping the tough El Paso gun-fighters in line. The young ranchman never dreamed of such a thing.

He remained on the Travis County range, and in the horse business, for nearly nine years. Then a small party of strangers rode through Central Texas, stealing several horses from this rancher, and a few more from that one, until in all they had made away with nearly a hundred animals from the general vicinity of Liberty Hill alone. They were careful to steal only from the smaller ranches and not to inflict any heavy losses upon one individual which would warrant his attempt to recover the animals.

The scheme had worked perfectly in other sections of Texas and surrounding states, but at Liberty Hill there was John R. Hughes, and he would not countenance theft of his property. Moreover, the robbers had taken his prize stallion, Moscow, which had won purses at the

county fair races in Georgetown, and also fifteen head of the range horses. The latter did not
bear his "Running H" brand, and therefore the
thieves had not realized they were annexing so
many from one owner.

It was a week or more before the ranchers had
compared figures to determine their total losses,
and almost another week had passed before
Hughes could act. In the meantime, he had
visited his neighbors and had struck a bargain
with them. He would go after the gang and attempt to recover the stolen stock, providing the
neighbors took care of his property during his
absence.

It was on May 4, 1886, that he set out to
follow a trail more than two weeks old. He
had an advantage in that he could cover more
ground in a day than the robbers, but the latter
had such a start that there was no telling when
he would be able to catch up with them. He was
confident that he could run them down by putting to full use the tracking lore he had learned
during his years with the Indians, and equally
confident that he could give a good account of
himself once he caught up with the gang.

Hughes traveled light, carrying only his rifle,
a saddle bag of provisions, and a blanket roll.
The trail led first to the northwest, across the
open range toward the Texas Panhandle and
through a wild, forbidding country broken only
by a few scattered ranch houses. As he had anticipated, he soon lost the hoof marks of the
stolen animals when the robbers turned onto a

traveled route. After that he could only trace them by making inquiries at the few ranches he came upon, or by hunting out their overnight camping spots. Frequently the trail forked. Then there was the problem of deciding which route to follow. Often he guessed wrong and lost precious hours looping back.

Days passed into weeks and then into months. But he never thought of turning back. At length the robbers headed south again. The lone horseman, sometimes a month behind, patiently followed. Across the Llano Estacado to the Pecos River they led him, and then to Magdalena, New Mexico. From there he followed down the Gila to the "Big LC" ranch, then south and east through Silver City.

If West Texas was a wilderness at this time, the territory of New Mexico was even wilder. There were few settlements and practically no ranches. Many of the inhabitants were outlaws—fugitives from justice in other localities. Many were murderers wanted for prosecution in connection with the infamous Salt War which had flared just prior to this period. The young rancher had heard about this trouble, which had started when a wealthy landowner had attempted to fence off the salt beds, the only source of supply for the Mexican *peons* in that area, and realized that he might run into some of these blood-thirsty scoundrels.

He pushed on, never knowing but what men might be lurking behind the next big rock, ready to murder him for his horse and equipment. He rode until his mount grew tired and then they rested, either under the stars or in a dry arroyo, the banks of which would shade them from the mountain sun. He shot wild game and fowl for food. Sometimes he hunted for a whole day, or a whole night, to find water fit to drink.

He had little use for money, except to buy ammunition, staple provisions, and new shoes for his pony. When his funds ran low, he sought work at the nearest ranch. He held several such jobs temporarily, quitting each one as soon as he had earned enough to carry him a few weeks more on his disheartening search.

During one such temporary lay-over, on a ranch in the deep interior of New Mexico, he was present in a little group around a corral when a wandering cowboy rode up with exciting news.

"Jim Courtright was killed over in Fort Worth," the stranger said, with the smug air of one imparting vital information. "Who do you think beat him to the draw? You won't believe it—Luke Short!"

The local men were acquainted with both gun-fighters from their activities in the territory. Jim Courtright, whose black, shoulder-length hair cast an aura of romance around him, was one of the fastest men with his pistols in the entire Southwest. Luke Short, on the other hand, was more of a rifleman than a pistoleer. He had fired his long gun in the Lincoln County War, with some success, but everyone knew he was nowhere near a match for Jim in a .45 showdown.

The cowboy had all the facts, and proudly related them. Courtright, a former army scout and marshal of Fort Worth, had opened a private detective agency there, and had tangled with Short, who was proprietor of a gambling house. It had been expected in sporting circles that the pair would finally meet to settle their differences, and it was a hundred-to-one bet that the gambler would fall the vanquished.

By some unaccountable freak, Short managed to fire a split second ahead of his adversary when they finally faced one another. His shot hit Courtright in the hammer thumb. Jim attempted to toss the pistol to his other hand in a quick border shift, but Short's second shot pierced his heart.

The cowboy, wound up for yarning now, next began repeating the gossip he had picked up in his travels through the territory.

"Seems like there'll be some more trouble down south pretty soon," he continued. "Some men from Texas brought in three or four hundred critters to start a horse ranch—I never saw so many different brands."

To frontiersmen, this meant that undoubtedly the animals were stolen property. Many ranches in the Southwest were first stocked by stolen animals, and there was nothing especially unique about that. But when the cowboy added that the horse herd was as fine as any he had ever seen, it was understood that the owners

probably would appear and that then someone would die. Valued stock was rarely surrendered to thieves without a struggle.

Hughes was giving full attention now. This
might be the lead he had been awaiting. He had
not revealed his true mission in the territory,
and did not now. But by skillful questioning he
learned the exact location of the new ranch, and
that the owners were headed by two men known
as the Renald brothers. There was no certain
indication that these were really the men he was
seeking, but he realized that he would never
be content until he had learned more about the
mysterious brothers. So the next day he gave up
his job, and took to the trail again.

He reached the new ranch in the quickest
possible time, arranging his arrival for daybreak. From a nearby hilltop, he watched a
small group of men at work throwing up an
adobe house. Finally he cantered up to the
group.

"Want to hire a good cowhand?" he asked
pleasantly.

One of the men looked him over. Suddenly
Hughes realized that—if his suspicions were
correct—the man might recognize the "Running H" brand on his mount. He whipped off
his sombrero and leaned back on his pony's
hips, allowing the hat to swing down and cover
the brand on the flank. With his other hand,
Hughes mopped his brow. The other apparently saw nothing unnatural in these movements.

"Not today, stranger. We've got plenty of help," he said.

Hughes chatted for a few minutes, asked directions to the nearest settlement, and then requested permission to water his pony. He rode to the corral, and found it full of horses. Suddenly his heart began pounding. There, near the gate, was Moscow, his pet stallion. His long search was over.

For an instant blind rage seized him. His natural instinct was to draw his weapons and force a showdown, but he was hopelessly outnumbered and he knew that if he gave the thieves a single reason, even for suspicion, he could scarcely expect to ride away from the corral alive. He curbed his anger, and, when his pony had watered, headed for the settlement about twenty-five miles distant.

Long before he had arrived there, he had formulated his plans and, luckily, he had no trouble in immediately locating Sheriff Frank Swafford. Mincing no words, he explained his mission and produced the credentials given him by his neighbors, which included complete descriptions of the stolen stock.

"I've heard tell those men don't look right," Swafford drawled. "We'll ride out tomorrow."

The sheriff, one deputy, and Hughes were en route at daybreak. When they arrived at the ranch, they found only two of the men working on the construction. The others were not in sight. Swafford identified himself, and the

two men gave their names as Renald—owners
of the outfit.

"Seems like you've got some mixed brands
out here," Swafford said. "We'll have a look.
Maybe this young man knows where some of
your critters came from."

Things began to happen instantly. One of
the brothers began cursing, and his hand flick-
ed toward his pistol. Before he could draw,
Hughes had him covered with the rifle which
had been resting across his saddle horn. Almost
simultaneously a shot came from the direction
of the corral. It sent Sheriff Swafford's hat
gliding from his head. Then the gun-fire was
deafening.

Swafford and his deputy wheeled their horses
and raced toward the corral, pistols blazing.
Hughes leaped to the ground and disarmed the
men in front of his weapon. Two more had
rushed from the interior of the half finished
building at the sound of the first shot, and
Hughes also took their weapons before they
could use them.

The battle at the corral was equally short-
lived. The two officers were deadly marksmen.
Before their weapons were empty, four men
lay in the dust. The last died before sunset that
afternoon. The only wound suffered by the
forces of the law was a grazed shoulder of the
deputy sheriff which was not serious enough
to require medical attention.

The Renald brothers, and seven of their
henchmen who had likewise surrendered, were

taken to jail. The following day they assisted in rounding up the stock from Liberty Hill.

It was a proud day for Hughes when he rode up to his Travis County ranch again, astride Moscow. He and the man he had hired in New Mexico to assist him, had brought back seventy-seven head of horses, which were returned to their rightful owners. True to their promises, the neighbors had kept up his ranch, and his horse herd was intact.

The young rancher attempted to pick up his work where he had left it, but life was different now. Word of his success, and of the New Mexico fight, had spread through Central Texas, and before he had been home a week, an officer from Georgetown rode out to visit him.

"Mr. Hughes," the officer said, "maybe you know some of those men over in New Mexico were friends of Butch Cassidy. I came out to warn you—you'd better take care of yourself."

Butch Cassidy was the notorious leader of the Wild Bunch, a fierce band of train robbers and murderers who had recently begun to terrorize the Southwest. This gang, and the Hole-In-the-Wall bandits, had been operating in the North Central states for several years. Citizens of Wyoming, Utah, Idaho, Colorado and Montana, knew and feared them.

Hughes had been aware of his position before the officer brought the friendly warning. The Renald brothers had been associated with a certain New Mexico bandit, he had learned, and this man was on friendly terms with Cassidy. To arouse the hatred of either was almost the equivalent of being served with a death warrant by both.

Hughes thanked the officer for his interest, and continued his regular work, taking only one precaution. To avoid being awakened in his cabin by cold steel at his forehead, he slipped out every evening and went up the canyon to make his bed under the stars.

As he rolled out of his blanket at daybreak one morning, about two hundred yards from the ranch buildings, he suddenly heard a burst of gun-fire coming from the cabin. Mystified, he drew his pistol and ran in that direction. Before he had gone far, he saw a lone horseman, crouched low in his saddle, disappear over the rim of the nearby hills. As he drew near the cabin, a tall, broad-shouldered young man emerged and ran toward a tethered horse. Hughes fingered his pistol and pushed forward. Suddenly the stranger saw him and halted.

"Are you Hughes?" he shouted.

The young rancher nodded, and awaited the next development.

"I'm Aten—Texas Ranger," the stranger continued. "A consarned cuss came in there to kill you, and he almost got me. If I'd had my boots on, I'd 'a caught him."

Ranger Aten then explained his presence at the ranch. A man named Brantigan had been murdered near the town of Fredericksburg some weeks earlier, and Governor John Ireland had assigned the Ranger to the case. Three of the killers had been rounded up, but the fourth was at large. He had been identified as one Roberts, a member of the Wild Bunch, and the Governor, who had heard of Hughes' experiences in New Mexico, had instructed Aten to visit the Hughes ranch.

"Roberts is a relative of a couple of those men who died in New Mexico," the Governor had said, "and maybe that rancher, Hughes, can help you."

Aten had arrived late the preceding evening. Finding the cabin empty, he had followed the custom of the range and had made himself at home. When Hughes did not appear, he fixed himself a meal. After awhile he pulled off his boots and went to sleep on the bunk. He was awakened just at daybreak by the creaking of the cabin door, and as he leaped up and grabbed his pistol, who should appear in the doorway but Roberts, the murderer he was seeking.

"He cut loose at me," Aten said, "but he's a rotten shot. I don't know how he ever killed Brantigan. I let him have it, too, and probably I hit him."

The two men quickly examined the ground near the cabin and found tell-tale stains on the grass where Roberts had mounted his horse. Hughes and Aten saddled their mounts, and took up the trail. About a quarter of a mile from the cabin they found a blood-stained sombrero, which led them to believe that the outlaw had suffered a head wound. Although they searched throughout the day, they could not find the body they half expected would be somewhere nearby.

Both the ranchman and his guest slept in the open away from the cabin that night. The next morning, at the urgent request of the Ranger, Hughes agreed to accompany him on the search for Roberts and once again requested neighbors to watch over his property.

They had no trail to follow, but by making inquiries at the ranches they came upon, they were able to determine the general direction in which the fleeing man was headed. At the end of three weeks they had followed him to the badlands along the northern border of Texas, adjacent to Indian Territory, where the Wild Bunch maintained a stronghold. Roberts had many friends in that district to give him shelter, and the two pursuers realized that the most difficult part of their job still lay before them. They had learned that one of the Ranger's bullets had struck the outlaw in the hand. This wound accounted for the stains on the sombrero.

The two men posed as cowhands and finally found work on a ranch in the neighborhood. There they heard that Roberts was "sparking" the daughter of a rancher who resided in the opposite corner of the county. They gave up their jobs and, traveling mostly at night, finally located the ranch and established a hide-out from which they could watch the cabin without being seen.

After making certain that the outlaw was not there, they made their camp some distance away. If he came a-courting, he would most likely appear in the late afternoon or evening, they decided. Therefore, there was no need of their risking discovery by remaining near the cabin during the day. But every afternoon they crept into their hiding place and stood watch.

More than a week passed, and they wondered if their information was unreliable. Then, about sundown one evening, they spotted a lone horseman coming up the trail. Instinctively, they felt that he was the man they were seeking.

"We'll head him off," Aten announced.

Keeping out of sight behind large rocks and brush, he and Hughes ran down the hillside toward the trail. They quickly reached a point about two hundred yards from the ranch buildings, and crouched behind a bush. The horseman was not in sight. Presently he appeared, his pony at a walk. Aten nudged his companion and nodded. It was Roberts. When he was a dozen feet away, the Ranger suddenly leaped out.

"I want you, Roberts!" he shouted.

The outlaw was riding with his hands in front of him. With scarcely a noticeable movement, he tipped his pistol holster and through the open end began firing at the two men.

His bullets kicked up dust behind the pair, and one tore through Aten's jacket. The Ranger and Hughes returned the fire, and Roberts toppled from his horse. He was carried to the ranch

cabin where he died, but not before he had confessed to the murder of Brantigan and to a long
string of vicious crimes.

When the usual formalities of such incidents
had been disposed of, Aten and Hughes rode
back to the latter's ranch. By this time they
were fast friends. The Ranger had already suggested many times that Hughes enlist in the
service, and on this return trip he painted stirring word pictures of the benefits and glory of
preserving law and order in a country where
fearless and honest officers were sorely needed.
Finally he got around to a point of logic which
bore considerable weight with the young
rancher.

Since Roberts had been a member of the
Wild Bunch, it was a certainty now that Butch
Cassidy would never allow Hughes to live in
peace at his ranch. If Cassidy followed his usual
course, he would arrange an ambush, and
Hughes would be "dry-gulched"—he would die
from a bullet wound in the back. If the young
rancher had to fight outlaws to survive, then
why not fight them in an official capacity as a
Ranger and for thirty dollars a month and ra-
tions—the pay for Ranger privates at that time.

"And why not?" Hughes asked himself.

At least he could serve for a few months or
a year. Perhaps during that time the Wild
Bunch would cool off, and he could then return
to his ranch in comparative safety. He told
Aten of his decision and the latter carried the
word to Austin.

CHAPTER III

JOHN R. HUGHES BECAME
a Ranger private at Georgetown, Texas, on
August 10, 1887. He was then thirty-two years
old. Governor Ireland, through Aten, had requested that he enlist, and if the Governor had
guessed what great benefits the state of Texas
would gain from this enlistment, he might have
sent a troop of cavalry and a band of trumpeters
to do fitting honor. But the Governor could not

foresee the future, and Hughes took his oath in the court clerk's office, with only that official and Aten in attendance.

He was given orders to join Company D, Frontier Battalion, then stationed at Camp Wood, near Uvalde and the Rio Grande border, about two-hundred miles south of Georgetown. He was allowed a few days in which to arrange his personal affairs, and then set out for the capital. As he rode through Georgetown he was stopped by the same officer who had given him a friendly warning on an earlier day.

"Take care, Mr. Hughes," the man said. "Butch Cassidy knows you're riding to Austin, and he's threatening to waylay you. Says he figures on putting a bullet right through your Ranger commission."

Hughes gravely thanked the officer, and headed down the trail. From long habit, and without being conscious of it, he scanned the horizon at regular intervals, taking note of every approaching horseman and team. He saw nothing to arouse his suspicion until he had covered half the distance to Austin. At that point he was riding through the most desolate stretch of the whole trip, and a small group of horsemen were galloping up the trail toward him. Moreover, his practiced eye caught the reflection of the sun on the steel barrels of rifles.

He thought of the friendly words of warning in Georgetown. It was possible—indeed it was likely—that the approaching horsemen were members of the Wild Bunch. Perhaps Butch

Cassidy was among them. They would out-
number him five or six to one.

By hard riding, he could have lost himself in
the hills at the side of the trail, but flight of this
kind was against his nature. And anyway, now
that he was a Ranger, it was his duty to engage
the outlaws—if they were outlaws. He un-
loosened his weapons in their holsters, and rode
forward at a leisurely pace.

Although Hughes was fearless, he was not
foolhardy. As he rode along, he mapped out in
his mind exactly what he would do when he
met the horsemen. By slowing his mount to a
walk, and carefully gauging the speed of the
approaching riders, he figured on being close to
a large rock at the side of the trail at the time
of the encounter—a rock which would give
him shelter and from behind which he could
hope to give a good account of himself, even
against superior numbers.

When the horsemen were several hundred
yards away, one spurred his mount and rode
ahead of the others. Hughes could see his swinging rifle as he galloped forward. If this were
Butch, could it be that he was riding ahead to
challenge him in a man to man duel? Cassidy
never had shown that kind of courage, but
still—

Then, suddenly, Hughes' worries were completely allayed. The lone horseman coming
towards him was none other than his good
friend, Aten. The latter had also heard of the
threats made by the Wild Bunch, and he and

some companions had ridden out to give Hughes a welcome, and assistance should it be needed.

If Butch Cassidy, or any of the members of his gang, had planned to waylay Hughes, they did not put in an appearance. On that day they might have been busy in a distant state, for they were still robbing and fighting in the north. Captain Hughes never met Cassidy, the Sundance Kid, Kid Curry, or any of the Wild Bunch leaders.

A few years after this episode, he learned that a large posse had left Denver on a special railroad train to engage the band of thieves in battle, and that seventy stock rustlers were killed in the resulting fights. Cassidy himself went to prison, escaped, and lived out his days a fugitive in South America. After robbing a mine payroll near Quechisla, Bolivia, he and a partner were cornered by soldiers. His companion was killed and Cassidy used the last bullet in his .45 to put a hole through his own head.

From Austin, Rangers Aten and Hughes were sent into northeast Texas, on the trail of a gang of bank bandits. Hughes had additional orders to go from that territory to Camp Wood. They had many adventures before they finally chased the robbers across the Red River, above Paris, and were ordered from Austin to turn back.

They were riding grass-fed ponies, and as they approached Paris, it was increasingly difficult to find that type of feed for the animals.

One night they camped in a graveyard, when they could locate no other patch of green. Both slept well among the tombstones. On another night they discovered they had pitched their camp at a spot where sandburrs were as thick as gnats. They moved their blankets to the center of the hoof-worn trail, and slept in comfort there, taking the precaution of throwing up brush barriers to keep from being run over by teams and wagons.

Hughes had ridden a distance of seven hundred miles with only overnight stops when he finally reached Camp Wood, and reported to Captain Frank Jones, commander of Company D. The camp tents were set up beside a spring near the banks of the Nueces River, a short distance below the town of Barksdale. There were no buildings there then, and no residents other than Rangers, but later Camp Wood became a flourishing trading center.

Captain Jones was busy completing arrangements to move his company to Rio Grande City, where the presence of Rangers was needed to keep peace in the tough border community. A wave of kidnapping had broken out there; bands of Mexicans were seizing their wealthier countrymen and holding them for ransom.

Before leaving Camp Wood, there were certain matters which Captain Jones wished to attend to, and as he sized up his new recruit, it came to him that here was exactly the man he needed to assist him. Hughes looked like a Texas Ranger. He was tall, broad-shouldered, lithe, square-jawed, and one knew instinctively that he would acquit himself admirably in any kind of fight. Moreover, the cool, steady gaze of his dark brown eyes—big, amazing eyes which dominated his whole appearance—told as well as words of his courage and devotion to duty.

So Hughes was immediately elected to accompany his captain on a series of important visits to stockmen in the general vicinity of Camp Wood. The "Free Grass War" was at its height in that locality. Already there had been several gun-fights, and more could be expected any day. Farmers were fencing in their acres with barbed wire, and the stockmen were as regularly cutting the wire to give their herds the benefits of the open range. The legislature, in a special session, had made fence-cutting a felony, and it was up to the Texas Rangers to enforce the law.

Captain Jones had a plan which he hoped might keep order around Camp Wood while his men were busy cleaning up Rio Grande City. It was a simple plan. With Hughes beside him, he interviewed the stockmen and told them in blunt language that they must obey the law— or else! The captain had a way of punctuating his words effectively.

"If there should happen to be any more fence-cutting in these parts," he concluded, "Ranger Hughes and some men will come in here to round up every last one of you herd owners. Hughes will do it, too! He'll bring you in dead or alive. You can tell that by looking at him, can't you?"

On several occasions, they narrowly escaped having to fight groups of tough cowmen. The latter, however, always decided in the end that they had better not draw their weapons if they intended to remain alive to boast of their valor. The captain was not bluffing—the stockmen knew that the Rangers were always ready to back up their statements—and the warnings had the desired effect. Company D moved to Rio Grande City in about two weeks, leaving the grass war at a standstill in the vicinity of Camp Wood.

Hughes soon had his baptism of gun-fire along the Mexican border. In fact, a day rarely passed without pistols or rifles blazing on the streets of Rio Grande City in duels of one kind or another. The young recruit quickly demonstrated that he was not gun-shy and within a short time drew a particularly dangerous assignment.

Catarino Garza, Mexican editor of a Spanish language newspaper at Corpus Christi, and a revolutionist who was plotting against the regime of Mexico's President Porfirio Diaz, the strong man of Chapultepec, had launched a bitter attack in his newspaper against United States customs agents in general, and Inspector Victor Sabre, stationed at Rio Grande City, in particular. County authorities, in an effort to prevent certain bloodshed, had issued a warrant for the arrest of Garza on charges of criminal libel. The task of serving the fiery editor with the warrant had been assigned to the Rangers. Garza was believed to have killed a half dozen men south of the border, and it was freely predicted that he would never submit peacefully to arrest. Hughes heard the rumors, and his lips were set in a grim line as he slipped the warrant into his pocket and mounted his horse to start searching for the revolutionist.

He quickly satisfied himself that the editor was not in Corpus. Then he received information which sent him galloping toward the village of Realitos. Garza reputedly was en route to Rio Grande City by a northern route, and the Ranger hoped to be able to head him off at Realitos.

He formulated his plans as he rode. Garza would fight—there was little question about that. Hughes was confident he could kill him, if need be, and by putting an end to his bloody career, contribute a real service to the state and to society. But if he took this course, he would be criticised. He realized that, as a new recruit, the public might believe he was endeavoring to make a name for himself by beating the well-known editor to the draw. Therefore, he decided, he must capture the fiery revolutionist alive.

Hughes rode into Realitos and dismounted in front of the general store. As he walked toward the door, intent upon making inquiries, three men strode out of the saloon nearby, talking excitedly in Spanish. Instantly Hughes recognized the center one as the man he wanted. Garza saw the Ranger at the same moment and froze in his tracks. A cigarette dangled from his fingers, held waist high and a few inches from his pistol. Probably he recognized Hughes. If he didn't, he was not left long in doubt. A lounger in front of the saloon got quickly to his feet. "Ranger!" he said, in a loud whisper, as he slid away.

Hughes, hands at his sides, started walking toward the three men. His muscles were taut. He was ready for sudden action. Not a word was spoken, but as he strode forward a strange hush fell over the street. Everyone in sight seemed to sense the tense drama of the moment. A few tiptoed stealthily toward places of safety out of gun range.

When he was a dozen feet away, the men on either side of the young editor fell back a pace or two. But Garza stood his ground. He stared into Hughes' eyes almost as though he were hypnotized. Eight feet—six feet—then only three feet separated them. The stare of neither faltered for even an instant. The Ranger halted.

"Catarino, I've got a warrant for you," he announced, quietly, calmly.

His words seemed to break the spell. Garza nodded nervously.

"Si, señor—I know."

Suddenly his hand shot to the butt of his pistol. Hughes was expecting this. He saw the movement the instant it started. He lunged forward and sideways, and grabbed the pistol as it was half way out of the holster. With a quick wrench he got it away from the startled editor, and in another instant had him and his companions covered. The fight was over without a shot being fired.

There was a buzz of amazed whispering in the courthouse at Rio Grande City when Ranger Hughes strode in with his notorious prisoner walking peacefully at his side. Garza pleaded guilty to the charges filed against him and paid a fine. He laughed, and most of those present joined in, when he was placed under bond to keep the peace. The bond would be violated—everyone was certain of that.

Outside the courtroom, the Ranger handed the revolutionist's pistol back to him. Garza took it, and then gave it to Hughes.

"Keep it—you won it," he said, earnestly. "I could never use it again. I would always think of my defeat."

Hughes carried the weapon for a short period as a second gun, and then gave it to a friend. He never saw it again.

Garza acquired another weapon, and when he remained in Rio Grande City it was certain that he and Inspector Sabre would soon meet. They did, some days later. They reached for their weapons simultaneously, but Sabre was quicker on the draw. Garza fell, seriously wounded.

Pandemonium broke loose. The editor was extremely popular among the Mexican residents of the town, and they immediately gave him their active support. Within a short time a heavily armed mob of at least two hundred men was clamoring for Sabre's scalp. Undaunted by the overwhelming odds, the Inspector prepared to fight. His close friend and brother officer, Tooney Dilliard, threw in his lot with Sabre. Together they gathered up a dozen rifles and pistols, several hundred rounds of ammunition, and barricaded themselves on the second floor of an adobe house.

As it happened, Captain Jones and most of his men were away on a scout, but a deputy sheriff located Hughes at a ranch a few miles from Rio Grande City and informed him of the impending battle. The Ranger sprang into his saddle and spurred his horse. He would stop the slaughter somehow, he vowed, providing he could get there in time.

The Mexican population predominated in Rio Grande City by more than four to one, and with two hundred or more angry Spanish-speaking men bent on destroying the customs men, there was no telling what kind of a riot might develop. Terrorized American business men appealed to the sheriff to quiet the trouble, but got no help from that source.

Finally the county judge, whose home would be directly in the line of fire, slipped into the adobe house and appealed to Sabre and Dilliard to change their plans and spare the lives which were sure to be taken once the fight started. Since they had plenty of ammunition, thick walls to protect them, and little fear that they could be burned out of their stronghold, they were not overly worried as to the ultimate outcome of the fight.

However, the Americans heeded the judge's plea, and finally agreed to call off the shooting match. Before the mob could charge, the customs men rode away on horses which the judge furnished, and safely reached Fort Ringgold, the United States army post at the edge of town. There they were placed in the custody of Colonel Clendenning, the commanding officer.

When Hughes arrived in town, the danger of an immediate gun-fight had passed. Armed sentries were patrolling the boundaries of the soldier encampment. The mob had dispersed and only scattered groups of Mexicans remained to argue heatedly among themselves. But there was an intense feeling in Rio Grande City which might flare up at any moment. As an officer of the law, there was only one course for Hughes to follow. Inspector Sabre had shot down a man in a pistol duel on a public street, and he must be taken into the county court to answer charges, even though such charges were usually speedily dismissed on the frontier. The Ranger mulled over the problem. He would follow the letter of the law—he was certain of that—but to take Sabre to court would necessitate parading him before the angry mob. Hughes realized that it would be a miracle if he kept his prisoner.

As it was after court hours, the Ranger waited until the next morning to go to the army post. There, he briefly stated the purpose of his visit and placed Inspector Sabre under formal arrest. Word of his intended trip to the courthouse with Sabre spread rapidly, and within a short time the streets were lined with excited partisans.

Hughes, preparing to leave the post with his prisoner, saw that most of the men were armed. To Sabre he said:

"I suppose we could circle around and slip in the back door of the courthouse. But I don't think you want that—and I'm sure I don't. I aim to show these people that there's law and order when the Rangers are here. We'll walk right through them. If any shooting starts, I'll give you a gun."

Sabre was not lacking in courage, and without further comment, they set forth. Scores of men stood along the sidewalks. A group of perhaps a hundred had formed in front of the courthouse. Hughes led his prisoner into the center of the street, and, side by side, they marched slowly toward their destination.

The Ranger carried his rifle in the crook of his left arm, his right hand on the stock to steady the weapon. The usual .45's were on both hips, and tucked into his belt was Sabre's pistol. Both men walked with heads up, disdaining to glance back to see what, if anything, was transpiring behind them. Hughes' dark eyes flashed defiance at the silent men on the sidewalks.

Before the pair had traveled far, a small crowd had collected in the rear, and was following at a discreet distance. Hughes and Sabre knew that if trouble came, it would be in front of the courthouse where sullen men were blocking the door. But the demeanor of neither changed. Neither slackened his gait in the least.

When they were a dozen feet from the threatening group, Hughes' chin snapped, and his left arm jerked slightly, causing the muzzle of his rifle to move a trifle suggestively. "Make way, there!" he shouted in a curt, commanding voice.

The silent men had had ample time to reflect on the sheer nerve of the approaching pair, and the order was as effective as though it had been accompanied by the snap of a snake whip. The leaders quickly divided and, in a few moments, the others had scrambled to either side until there was a narrow human passageway leading directly to the courthouse door.

Hughes and Sabre walked through the throng, shoulder to shoulder, and entered the little building. No one dared even to shout a threat at the Ranger, let alone make a move to seize his hated prisoner.

The law-abiding citizens of the town gave glowing reports of the incident to Captain Jones, but around the Ranger camp Hughes' bravery drew scant attention. He had merely performed his duty. On the morrow there would be equally dangerous work to be done.

Company D was in El Paso months later when the "Garza War" broke out, and other Rangers dealt with the fiery editor. His efforts at fomenting a revolution came to naught, and he finally fled to Central America where he lived out his days.

Soon after the Sabre incident, Company D camp was moved to Realitos, but the Rangers were back in the neighborhood of Rio Grande City the last of October, under orders to prevent bloodshed during the forthcoming November election at the nearby village of Roma. When the half dozen Rangers, Hughes among them, rode into the settlement, there was evidence on all sides that their services would be needed.

The Australian system of balloting was unheard of along the frontier. Politicians voted as many men as they could round up, and in Roma each of the two opposing factions had gone the limit in attempting to show a numerical superiority. Both groups had set up headquarters, in reality fortresses, behind adobe walls. The doors were guarded and the walls dotted with rifle port holes. *Cabrito, frijoles, tortillas* and *tequila* were served throughout the day and night, and once a male of any residence, or almost of any age, walked through one of the barred entrances, he could expect to be held in that camp until he had done his duty at the polls.

Word had spread through the country-side to the south, and *peons* were coming across the border in large numbers for a few days of feasting at the expense of the "crazy *gringos*." Roma had a normal population of about five hundred, but by election day there were more men than that behind the adobe walls at each camp.

It was not the Rangers' duty to control the election; theirs was the sterner task of keeping the rivals apart. Captain Jones conferred with the leaders, and finally settled his plans. One group would march to the polls election morning, and the other during the afternoon. The officers hoped this would prevent the bloodshed which would certainly result if the electorial armies met face to face.

The politicians of both sides sought the afternoon polling period, prompted by visions of annexing some of the morning voters to their ranks, but this was settled by drawing lots. The anxious officers patrolled the streets, and it is not difficult to imagine their relief when election morning dawned in a din of cheers—but no gun-fire.

By 9 A. M. the first group was prepared to march, and it was a picturesque procession that moved through the streets, led by gayly bedecked horsemen. Poll watchers from the other camp complained that some of the men at the front of the line slipped around to the rear to march up a second time, but the matter was settled amicably. Within a short time each man had slipped the ballot already prepared for him into the slotted box, and the Rangers had hustled all away to make ready for the afternoon marchers. The second performance also went off without special event.

Hughes did not remember which group mustered the greatest manpower. But he did recall that the Rangers rode back to their camp well satisfied that not a drop of blood was spilled. The bulwarks of democracy were unassailable along the frontier.

CHAPTER IV

IRA ATEN WAS THE FIRST, and the best, of John Hughes' Ranger friends, and each held the greatest admiration for the other. Their paths took them far apart, but for more than half a century they remained confidants, and frequently made long journeys to visit one another.

Had he remained in the Ranger service, Aten

undoubtedly would have risen to high rank and fame. He demonstrated that he was a top-notch frontier officer, fully capable of dealing with border outlaws, within a few weeks after his enlistment in Capt. L. P. Sieker's company.

On this occasion he had been sent with four other men to scout for a dangerous band of Mexican cattle thieves. Since he and Ranger Ben Riley were the newest recruits, they were given the pack drive detail, which meant that it was their duty to prod along the little burros which carried the camping equipment, and especially, to prevent the frisky little animals from unduly frightening farm teams that might be encountered along the trail.

It was customary for Rangers to scout with one pack donkey for each four officers. Heavily loaded with blanket rolls, bags of staple provisions, a dutch oven for baking bread, coffeepot, frying-pan, tin cups and dishes, the burros were grotesque sights even to humans as they clattered along the trails or over the range. But when a farm team hove in sight, they invariably kicked and bucked, as though they deliberately intended to scare the harnessed animals. Rangers made it a practice to ride in front of all such teams until they safely passed, to prevent runaways.

This particular scout took the officers along the San Ambrosio Creek, in Webb County about eight miles above Laredo, and finally the Rangers spotted the thieves on a hillside across the narrow stream. Aten, Riley, and Private

Frank Sieker who happened to be riding beside
them, took a short-cut across the creek and raced
forward on dry land. The mounts of their three
companions, however, bogged down in the mud
of the stream bed.

Riley was riding in the lead. "Texas
Rangers!" he shouted. The bandits replied with
a volley of rifle fire. One of the first bullets
knocked Riley from his saddle.

Aten and Sieker unleashed their weapons and
charged. Suddenly Aten heard a shout behind
him. "Oh my God!" He knew another was hit
and although bullets were whizzing around
him, he turned his head in time to see Sieker fall.

Aten gave particular attention to his sights
then, and his next shot knocked the rifle out of
the hands of one outlaw. The latter's companions had turned to flight after the first volley,
and now he followed. The Ranger continued his
fire and chased the thieves over the summit of
the hill. They streaked down the opposite side
toward a small settlement, where they later
were rounded up.

Riley had been shot in the thigh and was soon
back in saddle. Private Sieker, a brother of the
captain, died.

With this display of courage in his baptism of
gun-fire, it seemed that a great many of Aten's
later assignments ended in bursts of bullets. He
and Hughes fought side by side in the apprehension of the murderer Roberts, and were to
fight together on other occasions. On one sun-
shiny afternoon, Aten and a couple Ranger

companions lined up on the north bank of the Rio Grande in Dimmit County, prepared to shoot out a decision in an issue with four times as many Mexicans on the opposite bank. The fight was averted, however, when the Rangers and their adversaries rode their ponies into the center of the stream and signed a peace treaty.

Aten soon became a Ranger sergeant, and in August, 1889, was sent with two privates to attempt to settle one of the most desperate political feuds in Texas history, which centered in Richmond, seat of Fort Bend County. This assignment proved a turning point in the sergeant's career.

The Fort Bend County office holders at that time had been elected with the support of Negro voters enfranchised in the "reconstruction" of the district. As the fall political campaign approached this year, the old-line Democrats of Fort Bend publicly vowed to wrest control of some of the offices, if not all.

The citizenry quickly divided into two camps, and intense bitterness developed almost overnight. The office holders and their supporters were labeled the "Woodpeckers" and the old-line Democrats called themselves the "Jaybirds." A single Jaybird could out-fight a dozen Woodpeckers, they boasted.

Within a short time the two "coveys" had passed the stage of flapping their wings at one another, and it required no gift of clairvoyance to recognize that serious trouble was in the offing. The crisis was reached when two of the rival candidates came face to face in front of the courthouse, and each slapped his pistol. The Jaybird fired first, and the Woodpecker fell into the dust with a bullet through the heart.

As might be expected in this kind of a feud, a relative of the dead man buckled on his six-shooters and went forth to stalk the victorious Jaybird. He was successful in putting a bullet through the latter's heart, only, in turn, to be shot down by a relative of the man he had killed.

By this time the Fort Bend sheriff had realized that he would be powerless to end the bloodshed, especially since, from his position, he was a leader of the Woodpecker faction. He telegraphed word of the situation to Austin, and Sergeant Aten and two helpers were promptly sent to Richmond. It was typical of the times and the prevailing thought that the state officials were confident three Rangers would be sufficient to put down a threatened riot of several hundred citizens.

Aten did his best. He conferred repeatedly with the leaders of both factions, begging them to agree to a truce. But the issue was too clearly etched—both the Woodpeckers and the Jaybirds solemnly stated that there was only one method of settling the matter, adding the warning that he and his men, being outsiders, would be expected to stay out of the line of fire.

Aten was abroad early the morning of the showdown, and argued valiantly until the last. The Woodpeckers and their cohorts were lined-up in front of the courthouse when the Jaybirds started the march toward them. Aten was between the two groups, running from one to the other, arguing, threatening. When the inevitable moment arrived, he had no choice but to step aside. When the smoke cleared, eight men lay dead or wounded.

A couple of companies of militia were quickly mobilized and sent to Richmond to halt the warfare. The Woodpeckers and Jaybirds put away their weapons, but feeling remained intense. The county sheriff was one of those who had been killed and before the soldiers could leave, there was the necessity of finding a man for that office who would be capable of holding the two factions under control.

Sergeant Aten had demonstrated his bravery, and had been praised by both sides for his fairness. He was drafted for the post. There was a definite possibility that a new sheriff, regardless of his talents, might arouse the enmity of one side or the other and be put out of the way by an assassin's bullets, but Aten was not worried about it when he resigned from the Ranger service and took over. He handled these new duties with distinction for four years, and not once during his tenure of office did the feudists again unleash their guns. He ruled with a firm hand, but continued to hold the respect of all.

The young officer had long planned to retire on a cattle ranch, and upon leaving Richmond he married and took his bride to the property he had acquired in the Texas Panhandle. He firmly intended to devote the rest of his days to managing his herds, but men of his caliber were scarce, and there were many calls for his services in enforcing order. He resisted until the spring of 1893, when he heeded the pleas of his neighboring ranchers in Castro County, and again pinned a sheriff's star to his shirt front.

A lawless band of stock rustlers had all but taken over Castro County. Within three months he had cleaned them out, driving to cover those who were not taken to court or killed while resisting arrest. This accomplished, he again thought of retiring but there came another call which he could not ignore.

Rustlers were making big inroads into the herds on the famous three million acre XIT ranch in the Panhandle, and the syndicate owners pleaded with him to take over management of the vast pastures. He finally accepted the post, and held it for twelve years. Not only did he drive out the criminals, but he kept peace and order among the toughest lot of Mexican cowhands in the entire Southwest. They were impressed by his fearlessness, and especially by his dexterity in swinging six-shooters, and not one ever dared make a move against him. The manager who succeeded him was assassinated by a disgruntled cowboy in less than a year.

After resigning from the XIT, Aten took his family to California where he purchased a thousand acres in the famous Imperial Valley, and became one of the most successful ranchers in that rich garden spot. He was a member of the Imperial Irrigation District board, and helped win the fight against powerful opposition in Washington which made possible construction of the great Boulder Dam project.

His California neighbors discovered that his vigorous and colorful use of words could be counted upon to insure victory in almost any kind of an argument. His old associates in Texas had long admired his knack for forceful expression, and Dr. Walter Prescott Webb, eminent Ranger historian, discovered and preserved for posterity some of his most vivid sentences.

A short time after Aten and Hughes parted company on the trail, the latter to report to Camp Wood, Aten was sent to Navarro County to halt the epidemic of fence cutting which was causing serious unrest there. Upon the advice of his superiors, he and a Ranger companion worked undercover, and traveled into the assigned territory posing as farm laborers, and driving a scrawny team of mules hitched to a light wagon.

This mode of transportation in itself would gall any frontier officer, and the subterfuges of undercover work ran against his grain. But orders were orders, and he bowed to them. He wrote frequent reports to Austin, and some of them were recovered by Dr. Webb, while digging through old, dust-covered files of the Adjutant General's office. They are now preserved in Texas archives.

In one report, Aten wrote:

"I expect some of these days to stand up be-

fore a fire and shake off my six-shooter and
Winchester, kick them in and watch them burn,
and go up in the Panhandle and settle down
upon a little farm, go to nesting, be a better
boy, and read my Bible more.

"When I am called upon by an officer to
assist him in making an arrest, I will go out to
the barn and get the pitchfork or hoe and follow
in behind the officer like old Grangers do. So I
don't want to kill these rascals and have any
more deadly enemies on my trail than I have
already got."

In another letter it was apparent that the
Ranger was not as much concerned with his
future as he was in successfully completing his
assignment. He wrote:

". . . Nothing will do any good here but a
first class killing and I am the little boy that
will give it to them if they don't let the fence
alone . . . I wish I had Hughes to lay with
me on the fence, for it is awful risky business."

His final letter contained a statement as terse
as it was prophetic:

"These are my last fence cutters. We have
had to tell ten thousand lies and I know we
won't get away without telling a million."

He was correct—they were his last fence cutters.

He had devised a scheme for striking back at
the felons with dynamite, and when his commanders heard about it, they immediately summoned him to other duty. He had secreted a
rifle beside the fence he was guarding, and had

rigged it up in such manner that the trigger
would be pulled when the wire was molested,
thus exploding an improvised bomb.

Inexperienced in the handling of explosives,
he had used enough dynamite to blow up half
a county, so it was said, and the Adjutant General was on pins and needles until he received
assurance that Aten had dismantled his con-
traption, and that the frightful blast had been
prevented.

The Ranger was ordered to join Company
D, and soon after his arrival in camp he and
Hughes were sent on a scouting assignment
along the desolate border, with orders to capture, or clean out, a gang of cattle thieves whose
bold operations were threatening ruin to ranchers in that territory.

Border scouting was no play for children
during this period. Aten's earlier experience
along the San Ambrosio Creek was proof of
that. There were dangers and hardships every
hour of the day and night, which only experienced frontiersmen could face. And if the officers caught their quarry, a gun-fight was inevitable.

Captain Jones would have sent additional
men, although he sorely needed them for other
duty, but the two friends were confident they
could handle the job alone, and rode to the
ranch last visited by the thieves. There they
picked up a trail, and followed it toward the
wild, unsettled country bordering the river
boundary.

Following the hoof marks of horses which had moved across the range several days earlier required special abilities of the kind which Hughes had acquired in Indian Territory. Repeatedly he dismounted to examine a bent twig, or a tiny scar on a rock, and the decision as to whether or not the marks were made by the horsemen they were seeking, by other horsemen, or by wild animals or wandering steers, required the kind of judgment which came only from long experience.

The Rangers rode for more than a month, subsisting on what game and fowl they could kill, and sometimes going for days without bread or coffee. By this time the gang had discovered that the officers were searching for them, and had fled across the Rio Grande.

Tired, hungry and out of sorts, the two officers headed back toward camp to report their ill luck. Late one afternoon, they rode up to an isolated ranch cabin south of Realitos, seeking lodging and provisions. They were made comfortable and, much to their surprise and delight, were introduced to three extremely charming young ladies, visiting at the ranch from their home in Corpus Christi, where their father was a well-known banker and business man.

The girls were expert musicians, and one had brought her guitar with her. That evening the young Rangers and the young women held an impromptu song fest, which proved to be just the tonic the disappointed officers needed. Before the evening was over they had accepted the

ranch owner's urgent invitation to remain over
a day to join him, and the young ladies, of
course, in a fox hunt.

The relaxation and the mental stimulus of
such charming company was a rare treat to the
Rangers, and at parting, Hughes discovered
that he was smitten with the middle sister, a
gay, spirited brunette of twenty, whom we
shall know as Elizabeth Todd.

Hughes, alone and with Aten, managed to
pay several visits to the isolated ranch during
the next few weeks. Elizabeth encouraged his
courtship and, when he proposed marriage, she
accepted. He would resign from the Ranger
service before his wedding, he decided, and take
his bride back to his Travis County ranch, or
perhaps purchase a better and larger tract of
land in some other section of the state. But before they could complete their plans, stern duties
occupied his full attention.

One afternoon a workman ran up to a mine
office near the Rio Grande, about twelve miles
above Eagle Pass, and called excitedly that he
had seen a body floating in an eddy of the river.
A half dozen men raced to the spot and recovered the body, which proved to be that of a
middle-aged woman. There was no doubt but
what she had been the victim of a cruel, in-
human murderer. She had suffered a severe
beating about the head with some heavy instrument, and a large stone had been lashed to her
waist with a length of small rope.

County officials were hastily summoned and

they soon realized that they had a mystery on their hands. The woman apparently was unknown to anyone in the neighborhood.

Searching parties hunted along the banks of the river for possible clues, and, within a short time, made further discoveries which shocked the whole community and most of the state. One by one, three other bodies—those of two more women and a young man—were taken from the river, each plainly the victim of the same brutal murderer; each weighted down with heavy stones, tied by strands of the same rope, which the officers recognized as the type frequently used for plow lines.

The four corpses, all dressed in typical frontier apparel, were removed to an undertaking establishment in Eagle Pass for public inspection in the hope that someone would identify them. The first woman was about fifty, the girl about seventeen, and the other woman close to thirty. The young man was in his early twenties. Who they were or where they came from, no one could say. There were no identifying marks of any kind on the clothing, and the young man's pockets were empty.

Hundreds of citizens from near and far viewed the bodies, but none could offer aid. Finally the authorities wrote down complete descriptions of the four, then gave them a decent burial. The officers had not a single clue to work on; they had not even located the scene of the crime. It was extremely doubtful that the mystery could ever be cleared.

Ranger Aten, who was now a sergeant, and Hughes were working on another case along the Nueces River near Barksdale, about ninety miles from Eagle Pass. One day, soon after the murder victims had been buried, a courier arrived with a message for Aten from Captain Jones. It read:

"The authorities seem to feel that we can do something toward clearing up the finding of four murder victims in the Rio Grande near Eagle Pass. So I want you and Hughes to take hold of the matter and stay with it, regardless of time or trouble, just as long as you believe there is hope of accomplishing anything toward identifying the murderer."

The orders closed with a brief recital of the few known facts in the case.

The two men stared at one another. Here was probably the most difficult assignment they had ever been given. The victims had been buried as unidentifiable, and precious weeks had passed, chilling whatever leads they might dig up. But they broke camp within the hour and headed for Eagle Pass, hoping they might learn something there to shape the course of their investigation.

The written descriptions of the bodies, they discovered, were not of immediate value because there were few unusual physical characteristics noted. The young man's front teeth were widely spaced, and the thirty-year-old woman wore a dental plate, and had bunions on both feet. Other than these, there were no marks or peculiarities.

Aten and Hughes interviewed the officers, and the men who had found the bodies, but got little help from them. When they summed up the case, they decided there were only two courses open to them. First, as the texture of the stones used to weigh all four bodies was about the same, there was the possibility that somewhere along the Rio Grande they might find similar stones, and that such a spot might prove to be the murder scene. Secondly, there was the possibility that they could eventually trace the rope that the murderer had used to lash the stones to the bodies. It appeared to be new, and somewhere was the store at which it had been purchased.

The Rangers decided to follow the Texas bank of the river, examining all the stones they came across, and if they discovered nothing within fifty miles, they would return on the Mexican side. If this investigation was a complete failure, they would next set out on the trail of the rope.

Examining all the rocks along the river bank was a tedious job indeed, and they did not cover much ground the first day. Around the camp fire that night, Hughes suddenly recalled an incident that had occurred several weeks earlier. He and Aten had arrested a tough redheaded cowboy by the name of Dick Duncan for brandishing a pistol and creating a disturbance in Barksdale. He had been put under a peace bond. A week or so later he had called at the Ranger camp near Barksdale, and had spent most of an evening bragging about the gun-fighters he had known.

Hughes had not been favorably impressed, and consequently when he came across the cow-boy again on the range, he paid close attention to him and his companions—a cowboy Dun-can introduced as Picnic Jones; a pretty young girl Duncan said was his sister, and another young man he introduced as his brother-in-law. The party was in camp, and Hughes had noticed that they were traveling with a green Mitchell wagon.

"There might have been two more women nearby that I didn't see," Hughes suggested. "I don't remember, exactly, that the young fellow had wide teeth, but I might not have noticed. I didn't like the looks of that Duncan, though. I wonder . . ."

Aten wondered, too. They discussed the in-cident, and Duncan's probable character, at length. Hughes also recalled that the Mitchell wagon, which was almost new, bore the name "J. S. Clark, San Saba," stamped on the box. Obviously, "Clark" was the name of the mer-chant who had sold it.

Finally Aten reached a decision. "I'm going up to San Saba," he said. "May be foolish—but no more foolish than looking for stones along this old river bank. I don't like that Duncan either, and I'd like to know more about him."

The sergeant returned to Eagle Pass the next morning, then left for San Saba by stage, while Hughes continued his discouraging search along the river bank. Aten was the first to make progress. When he arrived at San Saba and called at the sheriff's office in the jail, he was informed that Dick Duncan was confined in a cell "for investigation."

"He came in here last night," the sheriff explained, "and claimed that people were accusing him of murder. Said he wanted to stay in until I could give him a clean bill."

Aten was perplexed. "What murder?" he asked.

The sheriff laughed. "Well, he doesn't know, exactly. Guess he means those four murdered people down at Eagle Pass, if those people happen to be Mrs. Williamson and her family from here."

Aten nodded. "That's what I thought," he said. "This Mrs. Williamson—who is she?"

The sheriff then explained that for several months, Duncan had resided on Mrs. Ida Williamson's ranch near San Saba, along with her two daughters and a son. Mrs. Williamson was about fifty, the sheriff said in reply to Aten's questions, while one daughter, Mrs. Levonia Holmes, was about thirty. The second, Beulah, was a girl of sixteen, and the boy, Ben, was about twenty-one.

Some weeks earlier, the sheriff continued, Duncan had purchased Mrs. Williamson's ranch, paying her $200 in cash, in addition to giving her a new Mitchell wagon which he had recently bought from J. S. Clark, of San Saba, and a team and harness. Then word had circulated through the community that the Williamsons were planning to move to Old Mexico to make their home, and that Duncan and a cowboy friend named Walter Landers intended to escort them there.

"They pulled out of here before daybreak one morning," the sheriff said. "About a week or ten days ago, Duncan came back, and asked Tom Hawkins, a blacksmith over here, what had become of the Williamsons. Everyone here thought that Dick had taken them down to Mexico. Well, people got to talking mighty quick. I'm glad you came, Sergeant."

Aten had heard enough. He was satisfied now that the baffling Rio Grande mystery was solved. But he realized that there was still much to be done before the red-headed cowboy could be charged formally with the crime.

He interviewed the voluntary prisoner in his cell, and pretended to believe everything Duncan told him. The cowboy swore that he had delivered the Williamsons safely in Mexico.

"If those people buried at Eagle Pass are the Williamsons," he said, "then some Mex must have killed them for the $200 I paid for their ranch."

The Ranger next talked with Tom Hawkins, the blacksmith, then started a thorough investigation in the community. Before he had finished, a message came by stage from Hughes, announcing that he, too, had made progress. He had located the murder scene—an old, abandoned ranch house, about a half mile back from the river, some twenty miles above Eagle Pass.

Leaving word with the San Saba sheriff to hold Duncan, Aten hastened to rejoin Hughes, hoping that incriminating evidence against the cowboy might turn up around the murder scene.

A less observing man than Ranger Hughes might have failed to spot the murder scene, he realized, when he heard the details. The private had kept faithfully to his job of examining the rocks along the river bank until finally his attention had been attracted to what looked like a "drag" on the bank—a spot where heavy objects had been pulled through the grass, possibly at the end of a lariat.

The grass had grown up again, but there were marks in the soil which the Ranger's sharp eyes had caught. He had followed the drag back from the river, to the ruins of the old ranch house, hidden in a small clump of live oak trees and thick mesquite. There he had found certain obvious signs that a struggle and murders had taken place.

Although the two officers searched diligently, they uncovered nothing in the immediate vicinity to link Duncan to the crimes. But when they broadened their search to make inquiries at the nearest settlements, they obtained important information from George Hobbs, storekeeper at the little town of Spofford. He distinctly remembered selling the new plow line to Duncan which was later used to lash weights to the murder victims.

Also, he had seen Duncan's Winchester rifle in good condition at the time he had sold him the rope, but some days later had noticed that the barrel of the weapon was badly bent. When Hobbs remarked about it, Duncan had told him that he had twisted the barrel while "handling" a frisky burro. However, W. W. Collins, a customer who was also present at the rope sale, had later seen the burro and had particularly noticed that the animal bore no signs of having been struck with a rifle.

The Rangers considered this vital evidence against the red-headed suspect. It was apparent to them that he had clubbed his victims with the rifle. But they still lacked the necessary evidence to take him to court. Indeed, they had not legally established that the four murder victims were really the missing Williamsons.

Their next move was to clear up this part of the problem. They obtained court orders to exhume the bodies at Eagle Pass, and then brought the sheriff and several former neighbors from San Saba to view them. The neighbors were almost certain that the victims were the Williamsons, but they could not be positive, due to the condition of the bodies.

The two Rangers had anticipated just such a situation, and had brought Dr. A. E. Brown, a San Saba dentist, to Eagle Pass. He positively identified Mrs. Levonia Holmes by the dental plate he had made for her, and young Ben Williamson by his widely spaced teeth.

Perhaps identifications through dental work had been accomplished in earlier cases, but this was one of the first instances of the kind in the United States, and Aten and Hughes were widely praised for their "brilliant detective work."

They now had a strong chain of circumstantial evidence against Dick Duncan, and he was taken to trial before Judge Winchester Kelso, in Eagle Pass. The missing Walter Landers was never located, and there were many who believed that Duncan had also murdered him, and had effectively hidden his body. The cowboy was convicted, and about a year later hanged for his crimes.

As soon as Hughes was able to lay aside his duties for a few days, he rode to the ranch near Realitos to call upon Elizabeth Todd. The ranch owner was the only one there, and he had sorrowful news. Elizabeth had taken suddenly ill and had died. The others had accompanied the body to a small town on the Gulf Coast for burial. They had tried to get word to the Ranger but he had been moving around the state so much while engaged in the Duncan investigation that it had been impossible to deliver a message to him.

The realization that he would never again see his beloved Elizabeth was a cruel blow to Hughes. Disregarding the expiration of his leave, he set out on a solitary visit to the secluded little graveyard on the coast. This was the first of many such pilgrimages down through the years. When he finally returned to the Ranger camp, he had decided to devote the rest of his days to the dangerous job of fighting outlaws. No need to think of returning to his ranch without his intended bride. The more dangerous his assignments from now on, the better he would like them.

Moved by this spirit of recklessness, Hughes volunteered early in the spring of 1889 for a job which offered much less than an even chance of his returning alive.

A relative of Captain Jones was operating the Fronteriza silver mine, at Sierra del Carmen, in the state of Coahuila, Mexico, about eighty miles south of the border. The mine yielded plenty of rich ore, but the owner had, to date, been unable to transport the silver bullion to the railroad station, 160 miles away. Mexican outlaws laid in wait to butcher the guards and make off with the shipments.

In desperation, the owner had appealed to Captain Jones to get him "three of the toughest men in Texas," to convoy the shipments. Jones mentioned the request at camp, and Rangers Bass Outlaw, Walter Durbin, and Hughes volunteered for the dangerous job.

"The Ranger service needs you men," Jones told them, "but if you want to go, I won't stop you. You'll be well paid—and if you get back, come to me and I'll re-enlist you."

As the men made out their resignations and prepared to leave, Jones called Hughes to one side. "I hate to see you leave, John," he said. "I hope you get back, because I want you in my company." He paused, deep in thought. "I want to warn you," he finally continued. "You know as well as I do how mean Bass gets when he's drinking. You'll have to watch him. If he starts trouble over there, you'll all face a firing squad."

Hughes nodded. He had been thinking of that very thing. Bass was a brave man and a great fighter. He would be a good man to have along, but only providing he did not drink. Hughes, a total abstainer, was determined to keep him away from alcohol, if there were any way within his power of doing so.

Word that the three Texas Rangers—ex-Rangers now—were en route to the mine preceded them, and Captain Jones' relative made good use of it. The very name "Texas Ranger" threw fear into the hearts of all bad-men on both sides of the border, and the mine owner saw to it that the word was given wide circulation through the mountains. The bandits would be afraid to molest his shipments in the future, he hoped.

The day after their arrival, the three Texans and five native guards left for the railroad with a half-dozen burros and five bars of silver, each one weighing about 150 pounds. The route they must travel was a winding mountain trail. The only signs of habitation on the whole 160 mile trip was one small village, Villa de Muchos, containing less than fifty people.

The terrain of the rough mountain country afforded many opportunities for bandits to hide until the silver train was well up to them, but the Texans, each an expert frontiersman, had devised a plan which they believed would forestall such a surprise. The native guards were assigned to accompany the burros. One Texan, usually Durbin, rode on the trail about fifty yards ahead of them, while Hughes and Outlaw fought their way through the brush on either side, swinging out at times as much as a quarter of a mile.

The two men on the flanks moved a short distance ahead of the main trail party, and it was their job to spot the possible hiding places of the bandits. They were confident that none would elude their sharp eyes. If thieves did swoop down on the burros, perhaps from the rear, the men on the flanks would be in excellent position for sniping, and they were, of course, expert riflemen.

The success of the convoy depended upon the ability and diligence of the flank men. If one were overpowered before he could give the signal, then the bandits would have almost a free hand in accomplishing their purpose. And likewise, if one of the flank men stumbled onto a group of desperados, he would have to fight it out alone while the others got into position to block an attack upon the silver.

It was dangerous, nerve-racking work, and the train made slow progress. This first trip was doubly arduous, for the countryside was all

new to the Texans. They were kept busy chart-
ing vantage points from which they could scan
the surrounding area and, what was more important, in finding overnight camping spots,
so situated in natural surroundings as to permit
approach from one direction only.

Perhaps it was the diligence of the Texans,
or perhaps it was the mere word of their presence with the convoy, that accounted for the
fact that this first trip was made unmolested.
Hughes and Outlaw had, however, many narrow escapes from savage mountain lions and
poisonous snakes. Several times they came
swooping down onto the trail with weapons
ready for action, only to find that the approaching horsemen were innocent travelers.

It took them about six weeks to make the
first round trip. The next one, also without
mishap, was made in a little more than a month.
After their third successful round trip, they
were given a few days of rest at the mine.
Hughes dogged Bass Outlaw's footsteps fearing
that the latter might start drinking. Apparently,
however, he had himself decided that it would
be best not to indulge. Finally Hughes relaxed
his vigilance.

Early one evening, while Durbin and Hughes
were sitting in their quarters, cleaning and oiling their weapons, they were startled by excited
shouting coming from the direction of the mine
store. They leaped up and ran outside just as a
pistol shot punctuated the shouts.

They raced toward the store, and through the

door window saw Bass, a pistol in each hand,
threatening a group of workmen lined against
one wall, their hands raised toward the ceiling.
He was weaving back and forth, intoxicated.
On the floor in front of him lay a workman,
dead from one of the silver guard's bullets.

To rush into the store and attempt to calm
the ex-Ranger before he killed again would be
to face his two blazing guns. Hughes moved
cautiously forward intent upon risking such a
move regardless, but at that moment Outlaw
began backing toward the door. With every
step he hurled dire threats at the men in front
of him. Finally he reached the door and halted.

"The first man who comes out after me gets
this!" he shouted, and sent a bullet ripping
into the floor.

Hughes and Durbin made themselves thin
against the building and when Outlaw leaped
out, they closed in on him, on either side. Both
were powerful men, taller and stronger than
the fiery little fellow. They pinioned his arms,
and twisted his wrists until he dropped his
weapons. Although he recognized them, he
fought furiously, and they finally had to tap
him on the head with one of his pistols. They
carried him quickly back to their quarters and
placed him on a bunk.

The two ex-Rangers realized that a mob of
angry workmen, clamoring for vengeance,
might be upon them at any moment. They piled
their weapons and a big stack of ammunition,
on a table and waited for developments. They

were three strangers in a strange country, and Bass was one of them. Even if the mob did not attack all of them, they could not surrender Outlaw without a fight, regardless of what he had done. To do so would be to lose face, and sacrifice their security. Contemptuous bandits would certainly attack them then, and they could not hope to get safely back to Texas.

They did not have long to wait. Presently a small group of men walked toward the cabin. The two Texans quickly extinguished their light, and Hughes, rifle across his arm, stepped outside to face the callers. Durbin covered him through a window.

Hughes, with a stern expression on his face, waited for the visitors to announce their mission. Finally one stepped forward, a mine foreman who spoke a little English.

"*Senor*, we come to tell you the men are not mad," he said. "Pedro—he was a bad man, he deserve to go."

Hughes' face brightened. There would be no trouble. He thanked the men, and they departed. By a special stroke of luck, Outlaw had killed Pedro, a man disliked by his brother workers. In his intoxicated condition, the ex-Ranger might as easily have shot a popular hero and precipitated a serious situation.

When he had sobered, Outlaw explained that he had shot in self-defense and only after the other had drawn a dagger. He was repentant, and promised his two companions that he would keep away from strong drink—at least until they were safely back in Texas.

They made two more trips with silver to the railroad. Upon returning from the second, they found the mine closed and padlocked. Clerks remained at the office, but the provincial authorities had decreed that no more ore could be removed for the time being. The Texans were paid off in full, and returned to Company D Ranger camp where Captain Jones, true to his word, re-enlisted them. They had been gone six months. Hughes and Outlaw were made corporals, titles which carried no increase in salary, but gave them rank when they were on assignments with privates.

One of Hughes' first orders upon his return was to round up a certain gang of cattle rustlers who had raided a ranch and reputedly killed a man attempting to save the stock. By means of shrewd detective work, Hughes learned that the thieves were members of a gang headed by Will and Alvin Odle, hard-cased cowboy brothers. He also learned that the gang's hideout was across the Rio Grande in Mexico, so situated in the mountains that a surprise attack was impossible.

He finally decided to recruit the aid of Sergeant Aten—and perhaps that of Corporal Outlaw—and make an attempt to raid the camp regardless of the odds. But before he could go through with his plans word was slipped to him that the two brothers, and possibly some members of the gang, were coming into Texas on Christmas Eve, less than a week hence.

By keeping in close touch with his informant, the Ranger learned exactly what route the outlaws would follow, and the approximate hour when they would put in an appearance, headed for a Christmas party at Barksdale.

Late Christmas Eve, he led Sergeant Aten, Ranger Outlaw, and Deputy Will Terry, of the local sheriff's staff, to a spot near the little settlement of Vance, where the trail forked. He was certain that the rustlers would come to this fork, to follow the main route into Barksdale.

Sergeant Aten was nominally in command of the expedition, but since it was Corporal Hughes' case, he allowed the latter to handle the details. Hughes placed Outlaw in a clump of bushes on one side of the trail, and Deputy Terry on the opposite side, while he and Aten remained in the clear where they could leap out and demand that the brothers surrender.

Aten and Hughes knew that there was little likelihood that the desperate Odle brothers, wanted for murder, would surrender without a battle. But the Rangers had stood together in the open waiting for gun-fire before, and each had the utmost confidence in the other's courage and ability to shoot rapidly and accurately when necessary.

According to Hughes' calculations, the outlaws would arrive shortly after midnight, during the first few minutes of Christmas Day. And his calculations proved correct. At exactly quarter past twelve, the waiting men heard the hoof beats of approaching horses. He hissed a low signal, made certain that Outlaw and Terry were ready, then took position beside Aten.

The moon was shining brightly, and soon they saw two horsemen coming slowly up the trail. Hughes recognized them as the Odle brothers, and nudged Aten with his elbow to convey the identification.

He and the sergeant waited quietly until the horsemen were almost upon them, then stepped simultaneously onto the trail.

"Texas Rangers!" Hughes shouted. "You're surrounded—throw down your guns!"

The startled horsemen drew in their mounts. For a moment there was complete silence. Then the leader moved quickly in his saddle. "Let 'em have it!" he yelled.

His pistol cracked, and instantly the air was full of flying lead.

The fight was over in thirty seconds. At the end of that time, the outlaws lay in the roadway, and their mounts were galloping wildly across the range. Will Odle was killed almost instantly. Alvin Odle died within a few minutes.

When news of the battle and the extermination of the dreaded brothers reached Vance and Barksdale, citizens prepared a note of thanks which was sent to Captain Jones. With the Odles properly disposed of, the message read, ranchers could breathe easier again.

CHAPTER V

THE BIG BEND DISTRICT, the great chunk of Texas land where the Rio Grande moves in a giant curve, was infested by outlaws in the early days, and the rugged mountain peaks and great stone canyons which were to become the principal scenic attractions of the Big Bend National Park, were known to officers then only as the almost unassailable strongholds of desperate men from both sides of the river.

Only the capable frontiersmen among the Rangers were assigned to duty in that vast region, so it was natural that Corporal Hughes, schooled in primitive living in the Indian country, should be chosen to assist another great officer—Ranger Sergeant Charles Fusselman—in keeping order there.

"Charlie," as the sergeant was known to hundreds of friends and admirers in southwestern Texas, had pitched his camp at Marfa, and policed a wide area from that central point. He was one of the bravest officers in the service, and mention of his name always recalled to Big Bend ranchers that June day in '89 when he engaged a gun-crazy desperado in a battle which lasted nearly twenty-four hours before the officer finally got his man.

As Fusselman rode into Alpine, twenty-five miles east of his camp, that spring day, he was met by Sheriff Gillett who informed him that a Mexican known as "Old Donaciano" was reported "on a rampage" in the little settlement of Haymond, about thirty-five miles farther east. The Ranger hastened there, by rail, and discovered that "Old Donaciano" had done his best with a pistol to blast out the windows of every house in the settlement. He had fled in a hail of bullets, and it was believed he might be found at his cabin at nearby Maxon Springs.

Fusselman borrowed a pony and rode there. It was dusk, and rain was falling as he approached the cabin, and in a flash of lightning he recognized "Old Donaciano" standing in a doorway. The gunman leaped inside, and started firing at the Ranger from a window. Fusselman let loose a few shots, then charged straight into the gun-fire. A bullet grazed his ear and another creased his high leather boot, but he got safely to the cabin door. "Come out or I'll come in shooting!" he shouted. There was no response.

The sergeant attempted to kick open the door, but the bars held. He backed away and charged against it with his shoulder. Four such blows broke it open, and he jumped inside, a .45 in each hand. The only occupant was a woman holding a baby in her arms; an open window at the back told the rest of the story. The officer wheeled toward the door, but the woman got in his way and it was several moments before he could get outside. By that time the gunman was streaking away on his paint pony.

Fusselman ran to his mount, and discovered that his saddle girth had been cut. He threw the saddle to the ground, leaped on bare-back, and gave chase. The gunman eluded him in the darkness, but at daybreak the Ranger picked up the trail, which led to a large patch of brush and cedars on a mountainside.

The officer quickly dismounted, and then began a deadly game of hide-and-seek. "Old Donaciano" and the sergeant crawled through the brush on their hands and knees, each endeavoring to catch the other unawares, and the exciting game, with death as the stake, continued most of the day. Finally they came face to face at close range. Fifteen shots were exchanged. The sergeant, in making his report of the death of "Old Donaciano," stated that he had put eight bullets in his opponent's body, five in vital spots. He was not hit.

Immediately upon his arrival at Marfa, Corporal Hughes began regular scouts through the wild territory between the camp and the river, sometimes with the sergeant but more often with one of the other two men then stationed at the post. He had been at the camp only about three weeks when he was left in charge of the detail while Fusselman, who also was a Deputy U. S. Marshal, went to El Paso to attend federal court.

The Ranger made his El Paso headquarters at the office of Sheriff Jim White. On the second day after his arrival, while he was sitting in the office chatting with the sheriff, a rancher from Mundy Springs, John Barnes by name, rode up to the courthouse on a lathered pony and ran into the office.

"Some rustlers just drove off half my cattle!" he announced, excitedly. "Half a dozen men there were, and they headed west. You've got to do something!"

Sergeant Fusselman leaped up. "Sheriff, you're busy with court," he said. "I'll take this on."

He and Barnes ran out of the office and were joined by George Harrel, an El Paso police officer, who agreed to ride with them. Barnes, who was unarmed, borrowed a pistol, and they rented mounts at a nearby stable.

Within a short time they had picked up the trail at the Barnes ranch and were following it up a canyon near the base of Mt. Franklin. It was apparent from the direction in which they were moving that the rustlers were intending to take the steers to the wild lands of New Mexico territory. Sergeant Fusselman was anxious to overtake them before they left Texas and his jurisdiction. He spurred his horse and raced through arroyos and around rocks until he reached the mesa. Then, in the distance, he could see the herd dust. He motioned to his two companions to hurry along, and urged his tiring horse to even greater speed.

The Ranger was riding a considerable distance ahead of the other two when the rustlers spotted him. A rifle bullet whizzed by his head and kicked up dirt behind him. He bent low over his horse and pulled his rifle from the saddle scabbard. He had decided that if it was a fight the rustlers wanted, he'd give it to them.

More bullets zinged by Fusselman's head, but he was anxious to close in. In a few moments he was within good shooting distance. He pulled in his mount and leaped down. He took careful aim with his rifle and fired once. Before he could repeat, a bullet struck him in the face, and he pitched over onto his back. His horse galloped away.

Barnes and Harrel were beside him in a few moments. They needed only one glance to tell

them that he was dead. Then they became aware
that the six rustlers were riding down upon
them. The rancher and policeman realized that
to stay and fight would be suicide. So they re-
treated, and a short time later rode up to the El
Paso courthouse.

"Charlie Fusselman's been killed!" they reported.

The news spread through downtown El
Paso rapidly and within a few minutes, two
dozen hard riders were on the trail of the murderers. But the rustlers were not to be found.
They had abandoned the stolen steers, and had
streaked across the border into New Mexico. As
evening fell, the possemen brought Fusselman's
body into El Paso on a light wagon.

It was almost midnight when the corporal
received a telegram at Marfa telling him of the
murder. Captain Jones happened to be at the
camp that night, and Hughes quickly awakened
him. The captain read the telegram through,
slowly, and then crumpled it in his big fist.
It was several moments before he spoke.

"You've still got time to catch the El Paso
train, John," he observed. That was all he said,
but it was enough. It was an order to Corporal
Hughes to set out on the trail of the assassins,
and to stay on it until he had found them and
avenged the death of his brother Ranger.

El Paso was nearly two hundred miles from
the Ranger camp, and it was after dawn when
the corporal arrived there. He immediately located Policeman Harrel and heard from him the

full story of the shooting. Harrel had recognized
a couple of the rustlers. The one who had killed the sergeant, he said, was Geronimo Parra,
a notorious border bad-man. The name was
etched into John Hughes' memory. Geronimo
Parra! He, Hughes, must live to capture that
man.

Sheriff White placed a posse at the Ranger's
command, and they were soon out of the city.
Hughes had decided against wasting precious
time by visiting the scene of the slaying. Instead, he led his men up the Rio Grande, on the
west side of the mountains. Whoever traveled
west into the interior of New Mexico territory
would have to cross the river eventually.

As he had anticipated, he and his men finally
found the rustlers' trail. It was apparent that
they were heading for some hide-out in the wilderness. Hughes pressed forward, even though
he was out of his jurisdiction. Finally the trail
divided. Each of the rustlers had struck out on
his own.

Hughes picked the trail of one horse, and
galloped after it until it finally disappeared in
the rocks of the mountain slopes. He split the
posse up into small groups, and each group
was assigned to follow one set of hoof-prints.
At the end of a couple of hours, all of the men
had returned to the starting point. It was impossible to follow hoof marks over the rough
mountain terrain.

The discouraged possemen were of the opinion that further search was useless, but declared

their willingness to remain with Hughes if that were his wish. The Ranger dismissed them and, alone, headed his horse into the bad-lands. True, there were no more leads to follow, but Sergeant Fusselman had been his friend and commanding officer. He could not turn back.

Only blind luck could lead him to the outlaw's camp in that wild country, he knew; so he confined his efforts to visiting the scattered settlements and requesting the peace officers of each to arrest Parra on sight. At the end of two weeks, he had obtained no clue to the murderer's whereabouts, except that he frequently was to be found around Las Cruces, a little town about forty miles north of El Paso. Hughes rode there, but Parra was not in his usual haunts. It was apparent he knew that the Texas Ranger was searching for him.

Hughes communicated with Captain Jones and received orders to return to Company D camp. The commander was as eager as the corporal to have the outlaw run down, but Hughes was an officer of the state of Texas and he could not spend more time out of his jurisdiction. And anyway, there was another important assignment awaiting him in the Big Bend district.

The young Ranger was reluctant to turn back empty-handed but he vowed that some day he would return to take the bandit prisoner. At El Paso, he made arrangements to receive word if Parra, at any future date, should re-

enter Texas. Then he hastened to report to
Captain Jones, at Alpine.

The important assignment which had been
awaiting him took Hughes to the little mining
town of Shafter, in the mountains of the Big
Bend, between Marfa and the border. An organized gang of thieves had been stealing ore
from the mine there for several months, and the
loss was running into large figures. The company had retained private detectives, but they
had been unable to stop the thefts, and neither
had two Texas Rangers who had been sent
there.

"I'm turning it over to you now, John,"
Captain Jones said. "I don't need to tell you
what an important job it is. The Governor told
me to put the best man I could find on it—and
I have."

Hughes arrived at Shafter two days later,
and discovered then how difficult was the task
confronting him. The mine superintendent had
quarreled with the officers who had been there
earlier, and was in no mood to give Hughes
co-operation. Moreover, it seemed apparent that
the thieves probably were Mexicans operating
from across the border, which made rounding
them up difficult. They undoubtedly had the
support of most of their countrymen at the
mine—and the population of Shafter was about
1,200, of which only three hundred, or less,
were Americans.

The Ranger was thorough and systematic
about everything he undertook, and, for his

first couple weeks, he did nothing but study the mine layout, and determine the probable trails traveled by the thieves. He also made a careful check of the mine employees and came across one name which caught his eyes. It was that of "Diamond Dick" St. Leon, an ex-Ranger who had been dismissed from the service for being intoxicated while on duty.

There was the possibility, of course, that St. Leon might have sunk so low as to be in league with the thieves, but Hughes had known "Diamond Dick" in an earlier day, and credited him with a certain strength of character. He reasoned that it would be more likely that Dick would be eager to redeem himself.

Finally he decided to trust this judgment. On one of his casual strolls around the mine shaft, he moved close to St. Leon and, hiding his lips with a hand, whispered, "Meet me in the old cemetery at nine tonight."

He strolled on, but when he turned and caught St. Leon's eye, he knew that his man would be there. And he was. Furthermore, Hughes had guessed correctly; St. Leon was eager to aid him. He was married to a Mexican woman, and had already learned through her the identity of the robber leader, and how they operated. Certain workmen at the mine secreted the richest ore in an abandoned tunnel. Then once a week, or oftener, men from across the river came with burros in the dead of night, and carried the ore to the gang hide-out.

The two men, safe from prying eyes and

ears, talked for more than two hours. Before they parted, the ex-Ranger agreed to do his part in the scheme Hughes had mapped out. So the next day the latter appeared at the mine office and asked the superintendent to discharge St. Leon. The request was flatly refused. The Ranger argued, but to no avail, and finally he had to allow the matter to rest. A week later, however, the superintendent was called away on business, and his assistant, who was more co-operative, dismissed St. Leon in no uncertain terms.

The ex-Ranger flew into a rage, and stormed around the office threatening to dynamite the shaft unless he was given back his job. He continued making threats outside, and a group of workmen gathered to watch him. Finally Corporal Hughes appeared and ordered him off the property. St. Leon remained defiant, in a way that awed the workmen, but finally left. Presently he appeared in a Shafter saloon where he announced that he had been fired simply because he was married to a Mexican woman. Then he proceeded, to all appearances, to become intoxicated.

Mexican residents of the town were sympathetic, and there were angry mutterings. Hughes had anticipated this, and had even considered the possibility that real trouble might develop. But he had decided to take the risk. Finally St. Leon took his wife across the border, and settled down to spend his days cursing *gringos*.

So far, Hughes' scheme had worked perfectly. Now he had but to pay nightly visits to certain prearranged spots along the deserted banks of the Rio Grande to make contact with his undercover man. St. Leon made periodical reports and at length brought the heartening news that his avowed hatred of Americans had so ingratiated him with the bandit leaders that they had invited him to become a member of the gang. He had, of course, accepted.

St. Leon gave him some additional information, and Hughes galloped off toward the Company D Ranger camp, to recruit assistance for the bitter gun-fight in prospect. Private Lon Oden, a brave fighter and a fine officer, was detailed to accompany him, and they hastened back to Shafter, where Oden remained indoors and out of sight.

That night the two officers crept up to a hiding place near the entrance to the abandoned mine tunnel in which a large quantity of the contraband ore was stored. St. Leon had given Hughes the word that a transport train would come for it that night, and that probably he would be one of the guards. By midnight the Rangers were chilled and cramped by the cold mountain air. They feared to move around; in fact, they dared not even venture from their hiding place, in case they might be spotted by an advance guard of the thieves.

By one A. M., Hughes and Oden were suffering real physical pain, but they bore it silently. At last they heard a slight commotion on the mountainside below them, then recognized the creak of pack saddles. The burro train was approaching. The question now was whether they would be too chilled and stiff to use their weapons effectively when the moment for the showdown arrived.

After what seemed an interminable time to the two waiting men, the ears and head of the first burro appeared over the edge of the grade. Five more burros were right behind, and with them were four men. Hughes strained his eyes, and finally was satisfied that one of these was St. Leon. This was encouraging. It would be three against three, if and when the gun-fight started.

The thieves seemed confident that no one would appear to disturb them. The burros were lined up in front of the tunnel entrance, and one of the men was left to watch them, while the other three went into the tunnel. The man who remained with the animals was St. Leon. Everything was developing splendidly for the forces of the law.

Hughes and Oden kept to their hiding place until one burro was completely loaded. They needed this evidence. When the three men emerged from the tunnel on their next trip, the Ranger corporal raised and leveled his rifle.

"Throw up your hands—Texas Rangers!" he shouted.

The thieves halted in their tracks. The two leaders dropped their loads, but instead of raising their hands, they yanked out pistols and fired blindly in the direction of the voice. A

bullet cut a twig close to Hughes' ear. He and
Oden returned the fire, and Hughes saw that
St. Leon was shooting at his erstwhile comrades,
and at close range. The two leaders dropped,
and the third dodged back into the shelter of
the tunnel entrance.

The firing ceased. St. Leon, whose marks-
manship had been the most deadly, fell back
to safety, shielding his movements by keeping
the burros between him and the tunnel entrance. Then he circled around to join the
Rangers, and to discuss their next move. Undoubtedly the remaining outlaw had taken
shelter near the mouth of the tunnel, where he
could fire, without making a target of himself,
upon any figure he saw silhouetted against the
sky.

Hughes ruled against an open attack upon
the tunnel, at least for the time being, and en-
deavored to prevail upon the third robber to
surrender peacefully.

"Come out with your hands up and you
won't be harmed!" he shouted.

The only reply was a string of Spanish oaths.

One of the robbers on the ground was groan-
ing. "If you care anything about your friend
there, surrender so we can give him water,"
Hughes called, in Spanish.

There was no reply this time. After a few
minutes of silence, Hughes ventured from
the shadows, and crawling on his hands and
knees, moved toward the wounded man. Regardless of the danger, he was determined to

give him aid if he could. He hoped that he might
be able to drag him out of range of fire from the
tunnel entrance, without being seen. He advanced cautiously. He had moved about fifteen
feet toward the prone figure when suddenly a
bullet kicked up dirt close to his head. Oden and
St. Leon immediately opened fire on the tunnel
entrance, and Hughes scrambled back into the
shadows and to safety.

There was another long silence, and then St.
Leon attempted to engage the robber in conversation. The man cursed him as a traitor, and
sent a bullet in the direction of the ex-Ranger's
voice. St. Leon returned the fire, hoping to en-
tice more bullets and thereby exhaust the thief's
ammunition. But the latter held fire.

There was no possibility that the cornered
man could leave the tunnel through another entrance, since the opposite end where the workmen secreted the ore was closed by a huge
boulder which required the combined efforts of
several men to move. Hughes knew this, from
his detailed study of the mine layout.

"Stay in there if you want to," he finally
shouted. "We'll come in after you in daylight,
and bring you out feet first!"

Several minutes passed, during which Hughes
was endeavoring to figure out some safe means
of raiding the tunnel. Then St. Leon stiffened
and leveled his rifle. "Drop your gun!" he
yelled.

The two Rangers realized that he must have

spotted the bandit. But where? They strained their eyes and couldn't see him.

Almost instantly a gun cracked near the entrance to the tunnel. The thief apparently had attempted to sneak away. St. Leon, who had taken careful aim, fired once and his bullet found its mark. The Rangers closed in. Two of the robbers had died with their weapons in their hands. The third was beyond aid, and died within a short time.

St. Leon, his job well done, slipped away before daybreak to take work which Hughes had arranged for him in a town many miles distant. His part in the clean-up did not become generally known around Shafter.

Corporal Hughes located relatives of the dead men the next day, but they would not claim the bodies. So he buried them, side by side, on a mountain top near the robbers' trail, and in such a position that on a moonbright night, the three white crosses marking the graves would reflect a grim warning to anyone venturing up the trail.

This ended the ore losses at the Shafter mine. The thieves on the company payroll were arrested and prosecuted. Hughes was paid a reward by the mining company—the main portion of which he turned over to St. Leon—and was also given a letter of commendation for his fine work.

CHAPTER VI

ALMOST ANY STRONG
young man, adept in tracking lore and capable
of facing and returning gun-fire without flinch-
ing, could qualify as a law enforcement officer
along the frontier in the Nineteenth Century—
and many such were available, for the border
country held a special attraction for that fearless breed.

It is difficult to understand, then, why a temperamental killer of the caliber of Bass Outlaw was allowed the authority of an officer's commission, even after his homicidal tendencies had become public knowledge. John Hughes never hesitated to say that the wiry little killer was not fit to be an officer, and he made the statement to the gunman in person.

While they were in Mexico together, guarding silver shipments, Outlaw confessed that he had come to Texas from his native Georgia because he was wanted there for killing a man. "Bass, you're not entitled to be a Ranger," Hughes told him. "You know you shouldn't be an officer—why don't you give it up?" The gunman offered no comment, and appeared to accept the remarks without offense.

Outlaw had been enlisted in Ranger Company E in 1885, and transferred to Company D two years later. He and Hughes were made corporals when they re-enlisted after their sojourn south of the border. The Georgian had several years priority of service over Hughes, and this was one of the reasons why he was appointed sergeant by Captain Jones when Fusselman was slain. Although Corporal Hughes was considered the most capable and trustworthy officer in Company D, he was detailed away from the company. Jones needed a second in command at the camp; so the job naturally fell to the little gun-fighter.

A week or two after his promotion, the new sergeant was left in charge when Captain Jones

was called away from the camp which was
then near Alpine. That same day, Outlaw rode
into town and began drinking in the old Buck-
horn saloon with Abe Anglin, an ex-Ranger.
Finally they began gambling with cards, and
the sergeant lost until at last his pockets were
empty. As he pushed away from the table his
eyes fell on the pile of bills in front of Anglin,
and suddenly his hand shot out to grab them.

The ex-Ranger, although unarmed, seized his
wrist in mid-air and held it in a vice-like grip.
"What are you aiming to do, Bass—take my
money?" he demanded.

They were on their feet glowering at one
another and, judging from his past record, it
seemed certain that Outlaw would slap his
pistol. A frightened spectator slipped out the
door and fortunately found Sheriff Jim Gillett
—Brewster County's doughty and greatly beloved "Captain Jim"—standing on the sidewalk nearby. "Quick, Sheriff," the man shouted, "Bass Outlaw's fightin'!"

Gillett ran through the door and jumped between the two men. He pushed Outlaw back
against the wall, and then led him outside.
"You're in command of Company D, aren't
you—and here you are brawling in a saloon!"
he exclaimed. "You ought to be ashamed of
yourself. Get on your horse, now, and go back
to camp—and sober up!"

The little fighter must have realized he was
in the wrong, for he meekly complied. But
the incident was not over. Captain Jones re-

turned and a day later called the sergeant before him.

"Bass, I told you that the next time you drank on duty would be your last time," the captain said, sternly. "Write out your resignation, now—you're no longer a Ranger."

Jones would not divulge how he had obtained his knowledge of the saloon affair, nor would he discuss the matter further. The sergeant obeyed, but he was seething as he rode into Alpine that afternoon. He was convinced that Sheriff Gillett had told Jones about it. One of the first men he met when he arrived in town was Judge W. Van Sickle, veteran Justice of the Peace, and he complained to him, threatening to challenge Gillett.

"Wait, Bass—I don't believe Jim did that," Van Sickle interrupted. "Someone else must have told the captain—wait here and I'll find out for you."

The little gun-fighter agreed, and the Judge hastened away, intent only upon warning the sheriff. With characteristic directness, "Captain Jim" immediately sought out the gunman and settled the matter.

"You won't have any trouble here as long as you don't make any," Gillett told him. "But I warn you—if you do start trouble, I'll know how to handle it."

Outlaw accepted the sheriff's statement that he had held no conversation with Captain Jones, and the matter was forgotten. The diminutive gunman moped around Alpine for several weeks, and then was appointed a Deputy U. S. Marshal under Dick Ware, the famous ex-Ranger who had killed Sam Bass, notorious train robber, when the latter had resisted arrest at Round Rock, near Austin.

Marshal Ware, Outlaw and another deputy arrived in El Paso on April 4, 1894, to attend federal court, and the little gunman was in ill-humor. He stomped around the courthouse complaining that Ware was unfair about dividing fees among his staff members. The other deputy had drawn a major portion of the fees and Outlaw was embittered, even though he admitted that the man might be entitled to them since he was the one who had worked up the cases.

As the day wore on, Outlaw began drinking and his acquaintances sensed that trouble was brewing. John Selman, City Marshal of El Paso, who had a faculty for guessing where his services might be needed, put in an appearance and began dogging the little fighter's footsteps. Early that evening, Outlaw swaggered into one of the city's notorious resorts, with Selman not far behind. The girl he sought was not then present in the first-floor barroom, and after a few minutes Outlaw wandered into the back-yard, which was surrounded by a high fence. In a few moments a pistol was discharged in the yard.

"Bass must have dropped his six-shooter," Marshal Selman remarked, and strolled toward the rear door.

Ranger Joe McKidrict, passing along the sidewalk outside, also had heard the shot, and he vaulted over the fence into the yard. He recognized Outlaw, and saw that he was intoxicated.

"Some sleep would do you good, Bass," he said. "Why don't you rest for awhile?"

The gunman wheeled. "You want something?" he snarled. He was holding a .45 in his hand. He quickly raised it, put a bullet between Ranger McKidrict's eyes, and another into the body as he fell.

Marshal Selman arrived in the yard just at that moment. Outlaw turned and opened fire on him. His first two bullets hit Selman in the leg, but by that time Selman had drawn his weapon, and he placed a shot over the gunman's heart.

Outlaw realized that he was mortally wounded. He dropped his pistol, scrambled over the wall, and started running down the sidewalk. Ranger Frank McMahon, attracted by the gun-fire, ran up and placed him under arrest, leading him to the back-room of a nearby saloon. Bass Outlaw died there, a man despised. Private McKidrict had been killed instantly, but Marshal Selman soon recovered.

Hughes was captain of Company D at this time, and McKidrict was one of his men. He ordered the private's body brought to the Ysleta camp, where it lay in state while hundreds of residents of the community marched slowly past the bier. McKidrict was a favorite of citizens throughout the border country.

On that earlier day, when Bass Outlaw had been forced to resign from the Ranger force, Hughes had been busy at the Shafter mines. Captain Jones had made him sergeant to succeed Outlaw, as one of Hughes' rewards for cleaning-out the ore thieves.

The new sergeant heard the full story of his predecessor's disgrace, and many times after that he and Sheriff Gillett were brought together in connection with their official duties. Hughes remembered "Captain Jim" as one of the truly great officers of the border frontier.

James Buchanan Gillett was the son of a one-time Adjutant General of Texas, and at an early age was enlisted in Ranger Company E, under Lieut. "Mage" Reynolds. He fought in a few engagements with warring Indians, and was with the Ranger party which chased a large group of marauding tribesmen across the Rio Grande and into the deep interior of Mexico.

Before he was twenty-one, Ranger Gillett had taken up the trail of Dick Dublin, notorious murderer, when Dublin had escaped from other Rangers, and had killed the desperate outlaw in a gun-fight. Gillett "kidnapped" another murderer from Mexico, became a Ranger sergeant, and a short time later resigned to become Assistant City Marshal of El Paso, under Dallas Stoudenmire, succeeding him when the latter was ousted from office. Although he kept order among many of the toughest gun-fighters of the Southwest, Gillett was never forced to kill a man while holding this post.

Later he became sheriff of Brewster County. Then he purchased the Barrel Springs ranch on Valentine Flat, northeast of Marfa, became a bank director, and at the time of his death was one of the most successful and respected men in the Big Bend district. He was never a Ranger captain, and the title given him in later years was purely honorary.

Following his promotion to sergeant, John Hughes was granted a short leave. Part of it he spent in contacting informers who might tell him the whereabouts of Geronimo Parra, the Fusselman slayer. The rest he devoted to one of his annual pilgrimages to the grave of Elizabeth Todd, the girl who would have been his bride had she lived.

Upon his return to Company D camp, he discovered that the bandit gang across the border had marked him for death as a result of the mine battle. One of the men who had died at Shafter was Matilde Carrasco, brother of Antonio, the cruel leader of the gang. Friendly Mexicans had reported to Captain Jones that Antonio Carrasco had ordered his fiercest killers to cross the river and bring back Hughes' scalp. To the one who succeeded, the bandit chieftain had promised five hundred head of cattle, plus a handsome cash gift of *pesos*.

"Take care of yourself," Jones admonished

his new sergeant. "The Ranger force can't afford to lose you."

Hughes was well capable of taking care of himself, and the captain knew it. In fact, threats against his life were nothing new to the tall young officer. He went about his duties much as he had before. The assassins would strike at night, if at all, he knew, and they probably would plot to shoot him in the back while he rode along the trail. So at night he abandoned the beaten path, and rode over the range. Two or three times he surprised men in ambush, and knew that they were waiting for him. He chased them back to the river with gun-fire, but made no special effort to capture or wound them.

During this period, Hughes was searching for one Desidario Duran, who was accused of a raid upon a section house. At last he traced Duran to his hiding place in the San Antonio Colony, a little Mexican settlement on the Texas bank of the Rio Grande, and with Rangers Oden and Jim Putman, went to make the arrest. Ordinarily Hughes would have seized the prisoners without help, but Duran was among friends and while the sergeant felt that he could make the arrest himself, he would need help in getting his prisoner safely back to camp.

The three officers made the arrest without event, and then stopped at the little store in the settlement, presumably to purchase fresh provisions. They were not in special need of any, and they would have preferred to hustle their prisoner away before his friends could rally to his support, but a stop of this kind in enemy territory was part of the Ranger psychology. Such bravado had its effect.

As the officers dismounted, three men left a side door of the store, and hastened toward their ponies tethered a short distance away. Two of the men were aiding the third who apparently was intoxicated. The officers watched them, with no special interest, but as they mounted their horses, the center man turned so that the Rangers got a look at his full face.

"That's Florencio Carrasco!" Oden shouted.

The Ranger had had dealings with the man before, and knew that he was another brother of the treacherous Antonio Carrasco.

"Stay with Duran," Hughes ordered Putman, and he and Oden sprang into their saddles to pursue the trio.

The race was an even one for a few minutes, but the Rangers had the better mounts, and began closing in. Suddenly Carrasco pulled in his pony, as though he intended to surrender. But when Oden, who was riding ahead, was almost upon him, the bandit opened fire with his pistol. His first bullet hit Oden's horse, and killed the animal.

Oden scrambled to a firing position and cut loose with his weapon. One of his bullets knocked Carrasco out of the saddle.

Hughes leaped off his horse to take the wounded man prisoner, but the latter still wanted to fight and turned a rifle upon the officers. Both Oden and Hughes fired. Carrasco died a few minutes later.

The gun shots aroused the residents of the little settlement and brought them running from their cabins. Some of them were members of the Carrasco gang. A hostile group swarmed around Ranger Putman, who was guarding Duran, and Hughes and Oden reached his side just in time. The officers were outnumbered, ten to one, but they stood their ground, and no serious trouble developed.

Realizing that they undoubtedly would be ambushed along the trail back to camp, Hughes led his companions and the prisoner out of the settlement on the main route, then took to the open range, following a longer but safer route back to Alpine headquarters.

Sergeant Hughes had no more than made his report to Captain Jones when an informer from across the river brought word that now Antonio Carrasco was shouting for all to hear that he lived only to see Hughes assassinated. He had threatened his killers with dire punishments if they did not succeed in waylaying the Ranger. If his men failed him, he swore that he would cross the river and do the job himself.

These threats had no more effect upon the sergeant than the earlier ones. He had always taken care of himself in the best way he knew how, and his way had been good enough to keep him alive for many years in a wild, unsettled country in which few good peace officers lived to see streaks of gray in their hair.

During the next several weeks Hughes flushed men in ambush every few nights, and had many narrow escapes. He sent a couple of Carrasco's toughest would-be assassins back to the bandit stronghold in burial boxes, and saw to it that the bandit leader knew that he was ready to deal in a similar fashion with the rest of the gang.

This brought a lull—the killers were afraid to cross the border. And soon it became apparent that the Ranger, single-handedly, had put an end to the criminal activities of the Carrascos on the Texas side of the Rio Grande—at least for the present.

CHAPTER VII

RANGER CAPTAIN Frank Jones was one of the bravest officers along the Texas frontier, but unfortunately his career was abruptly ended before the historians of that early day had compiled accounts of his many exploits. Succeeding generations quickly forgot and soon only a few of his friends and associates remained alive to speak the words of praise which were his due. John Hughes was one of those who knew him best, and who always gave him the greatest credit as a brave man, a good man, and a fine officer.

Jones was born in Austin, and soon after his twenty-first birthday enlisted in the Ranger force as a private in Company D. This was on July 28, 1881. His bravery and talents as an officer won him speedy promotion to a corporal's post, then he became sergeant of the company and finally captain, on July 15, 1886.

A fearless man himself, he required that the men around him give no thought to the dangers confronting them. Hughes had nerves of steel, and perhaps that was one of the reasons why the captain admired him. Judge Van Sickle, of Alpine, once questioned Jones' judgment in assigning Hughes, alone, to march half a dozen tough Mexican bandits from the Ranger camp to jail. The captain laughed.

"Why, Hughes could handle fifty men like them," he said. "He's a fighter. If they start trouble he'll kill them all, and come out of it without a scratch."

As a young Ranger, Captain Jones helped quiet the "Dutch War," at Mason, but his most spectacular work was done fighting the gangs of train robbers which made railroading a perilous career in West Texas. The crew of a Southern Pacific, G. H. & S. A. passenger train was threatened with a hold-up along a lonely stretch of track near Comstock, in Val Verde County, early in September, 1889, and an urgent call for help was received at the Ranger camp. Captain Jones and five men hastened to the scene by special train. Hughes, Durbin and Bass Outlaw were in Mexico during this period, or they might have been included in the posse.

The robbers' trail led toward the Rio Grande and Mexico. When the officers followed it to a point near the river, they discovered that the bandits had tried a trick used by many frontier outlaws. They had removed the shoes from their mounts, to make tracking difficult, and then had split up, each rider going in a different direction. Jones was experienced in solving such a ruse. He personally picked out one set of hoof-prints, and followed them until they finally brought him to the rendezvous where the robbers had reassembled.

The officers remained on the trail for six days and finally traced the bandits across the border and established that they had fled into the interior. While international boundaries seldom stopped Rangers in pursuit of outlaws, this time Captain Jones ordered his men to turn back.

One of the most sensational train robberies in the Big Bend country occurred in the fall of 1891, when six bandits held up and terrorized the passengers of a G. H. & S. A. train on Horseshoe Curve, a short distance east of Sanderson, and escaped with $50,000 cash loot from the express car. Hughes was stationed at Shafter at this time. Jones and the men in camp with him were delayed in reaching the scene and the robbers' trail had been destroyed. Undaunted, they spread out across the range, and finally cut the trail which led in the direction always taken by border bandits—toward Mexico.

At the end of several days tracking, the Rangers located the gang's permanent camp in the center of a canebrake in the desolate region on the Mexican side of the Rio Grande. By instinct Jones would have led his men in a charge, but as a Ranger commander he could not endanger lives in a reckless manner. And a charge would be reckless, for the cane would hide the outlaws, while the officers would be easy targets.

The captain stationed his men around the patch, and then set it afire. The outlaws braved the smoke and managed to slip away, leaving behind about one hundred head of stolen stock. The Rangers picked up the trail again, followed it back into Texas, and kept on it for nearly a month. At last they caught up with the gang, not far from the town of Ozona.

The thieves rode into an arroyo, dismounted, and opened fire with rifles, but the fight was soon over. One Ranger suffered a minor wound in the arm. Two robbers were killed, three wounded, and John Flint, reputed leader of the gang, hastily scribbled his will on the back of an envelope and died a suicide.

The wounded men recovered and were tried and convicted, but they would not reveal the whereabouts of the $50,000 loot. It was reported that the money had been hidden in the mountains of the Big Bend, and from time to time during the next fifty years expeditions were organized to search for it. If it was ever recovered, no public announcement was made. Bass Outlaw, among others, spent weeks hunting for the hiding place, following his discharge from the Ranger force. It is certain that he was not successful.

Gossip is still heard along the border to the effect that Flint did not kill himself; that in reality one of the possemen forced him to write a will and then murdered him, and escaped with the $50,000. The story was based on the fact that his body was found some distance from the others, and the additional claim that one of the possemen was a stranger in the neighborhood, and that he disappeared within a few weeks.

Hughes had ample proof that this gossip was false and malicious; that the entire incident occurred exactly as Captain Jones detailed it in his report. The maligned posseman was well known to Jones, and moreover he was standing at the captain's side at the time the gang leader died. The Ranger commander's integrity was unquestionable and he definitely exonerated every man in his party.

A desperate band of criminals known as the Olguins had been spreading terror on the Texas side of the border in El Paso County, in the vicinity of Ysleta and San Elizario, and in the spring of 1893, Captain Jones received a message from Austin suggesting that he take four Ranger privates to that section and quiet the trouble. Sergeant Hughes was to remain at Alpine with a small detail, to keep order in the Big Bend. Jones realized what this new assignment entailed, and in his reply to the Adjutant General wrote:

"If I am sent back to El Paso County I hope you can allow me to take more than four men. Old residenters say that four men will simply be murdered and will do no good . . . there must be fully fifty men in the gang that has caused so much trouble, and they are well organized, too."

His views received due consideration at the Capitol, but reinforcements were unavailable. Ranger Companies A, B, and C, were needed in other sections of the state, and it was likewise imperative that a detail of Company D be kept at Alpine. So Jones and the four men departed, early in June. He also was accompanied by his wife, the beautiful daughter of Col. George Wythe Baylor, former Frontier Battalion Ranger commander. Her earlier marriage had ended in a divorce from James B. Gillett, the sheriff at Alpine.

Jones quickly learned that his estimate that there were fifty members of the Olguin gang was too conservative, if anything. The real leader was Clato Olguin, an old man. His three sons, Jesus Maria, Antonio, and Pedro, directed most of the outlaw activities. They had killed

four men in the Salt War, and the number of
their victims since then was beyond counting.

Their stronghold was located at a little settlement called *Tres Jacales*—Three Huts—on
"Pirate Island," a little strip of no-man's land
south of El Paso. The original boundary between Mexico and the United States had been
set as the bed of the Rio Grande in that area.
But in 1854 the channel of the river had shifted
southward, leaving a little part of Mexico on
the northern side. Neither Mexico nor the United
States claimed jurisdiction over the land, and it
soon became a hide-out for the lawless, who
took up with the Olguins.

Captain Jones made his camp at the town of
Ysleta, about twelve miles below El Paso, and
conducted several successful forays against raiding members of the gang. Finally he prevailed
upon a local judge to give him a warrant for
one of the Olguin brothers—Jesus Maria—
and with Corporal Karl Kirchner, three
Rangers, and Deputy Sheriff R. E. Bryant, set
out to serve it. There would be a fight, the
captain realized, and that was why he took his
full force with him.

The little party slipped away from Ysleta,
and camped near the town of San Elizario. Before daybreak they were underway again, and
rode straight across Pirate Island to the Olguin
ranch. No one was stirring there when the officers came within sight. Captain Jones deployed
his men around the buildings, then signalled the
order to charge. He and Kirchner crashed

through the front door of the cabin, with guns drawn and expecting a fight. But the only person inside was Clato Olguin, the old father. He was sitting peacefully in a chair, as though he had been expecting his unannounced callers.

It was apparent that the sons had been tipped off about the raid, and had gone into hiding. Captain Jones led his disappointed men back toward their camp. They rode in silence for two or three miles. Suddenly they spied two horsemen slowly moving across the plain, to their left. Deputy Sheriff Bryant reined in his horse.

"One of those is the Olguin we want!" he declared.

The officers galloped toward the pair. The latter continued their leisurely pace, as though they were unaware of any other riders, although they must have heard the pounding hoofs. Had the Rangers but thought of this, it would have been obvious to them that the men were playing a treacherous game.

When the officers were less than a hundred yards distant, the pair suddenly spurred their horses, and streaked toward a little group of buildings around a corral, a quarter of a mile away.

Jones and his men had fleet ponies, but the Olguins were equally well mounted. They reached the buildings first, and disappeared around one. The Rangers charged after them; Captain Jones was in the lead. As they rode past the corral there was a signal shot, and then rifles blazed from all sides. The Rangers had ridden into an ambush.

It was apparent that at least a dozen riflemen were shooting at them. But it was not in Captain Jones' code to retreat. He and his men leaped to the ground and, using their ponies as shields, returned the fire. But the enemy was well barricaded. The Rangers could not spot a single human target at which to aim.

Captain Jones had halted less than thirty feet from one of the buildings, in which most of the gunmen seemed to be secreted. A bullet ripped into the captain's thigh, and he crumpled to the ground. His horse galloped away. Corporal Kirchner reached his side just as the gallant commander straightened his broken leg in front of him, and resumed his fire. The next instant a bullet struck him in the chest, and he fell backwards.

"I'm shot to pieces—I'm killed," Jones gasped. Then he valiantly raised himself on one elbow, and took aim with his rifle again.

Bullets were raining around Kirchner as he crouched beside his captain but, miraculously, he was not hit.

"Retreat!" Jones ordered. His head sagged. He snapped it up, and tried to steady his rifle. But the effort was too much. The weapon dropped and Captain Jones fell back dead.

Corporal Kirchner looked around him. If he and the others could find some kind of shelter, they might have a chance. Bullets were not coming so fast now, and the corporal ran to join his companions. As an individual Ranger, it was his duty, and his wish, to fight the outlaws until he fell. Captain Jones, however, had given him orders to retreat; it also was his duty to obey these orders.

Kirchner and the four others fell back a safe distance, and then halted. It would be suicide to charge again. But they could not bring themselves to abandon their dead leader. Finally, however, they made the only decision open to them. They were, after all, on Mexican soil. They returned to Texas.

Sergeant Hughes, now the ranking officer of Company D, received word of the tragedy in a telegram from Corporal Kirchner. The message stated that a hundred armed men were on the Texas bank of the river, ready to go after the captain's body, but that Mexican authorities from Juarez had taken charge across the border. Any acts of violence now would mean warfare between the two nations.

Hughes immediately broke camp at Alpine, and loaded his men and their horses into box cars, bound for El Paso. By the time he arrived there, diplomatic messages were flying back and forth from Mexico City. President Diaz was a member of the Masonic Order, and so had been Jones. This oiled the machinery and the remains of the brave officer who had died on foreign soil were soon sent back to his native land. Sergeant Hughes, personally, regained possession of the slain man's weapons, and other belongings.

It was several weeks, however, before the incident was closed. M. Romero, Minister from Mexico, made formal complaint to the United States government against the invasion of Mexican territory by an armed force from the state of Texas, and the Hon. W. Q. Gresham, Secretary of State at Washington, demanded an explanation from Governor J. S. Hogg. The Governor made inquiries from Adjutant General W. H. Mabry who, in turn, asked for statements from the Ranger witnesses.

It was Hughes who started the investigation moving in the opposite direction. Captain Jones, a citizen of the United States, had been ambushed and murdered by a gang of Mexican criminals, he pointed out. What steps did the government of Mexico intend taking toward punishing the gunmen? His inquiries, forwarded back along the line, finally ended the diplomatic discussions.

Captain Jones' body was brought across the Rio Grande on the morning of July 4, 1893, five days after his death, and on the afternoon of that same July Fourth, Sergeant Hughes was appointed Captain of Company D, by Governor Hogg. It was a great honor for the young officer, but a sad occasion just the same, coming as it did.

Hughes was thirty-eight years old, and he had been a Ranger just short of six years. His promotion was greatly applauded, both in the Ranger force and among civilians along the border. His courage and capabilities were well known, and his devotion to duty was a byword among his associates.

Tall, lithe, physically powerful, handsome, he was a perfect Ranger type in appearance. And he had an abundance of the other attributes of a successful commander. He was an expert horseman, quick-moving and quick-thinking at all times, a superior marksman, a shrewd appraiser of character, and unexcelled as a tracker and frontiersman.

Hughes did not smoke, drink or gamble, and in that respect was unique among the border men, yet it never occurred to his companions that he was not thoroughly of their kind. If he had faults, they did not recognize them. If they found him irritable, it was only when they had failed to follow orders to the letter, or had fallen down on an assignment.

His boyhood friends among the Indians had taught him the wisdom of keeping his own counsel; in fact, he exhibited many of the redman's traits in his every-day living. He was hesitant about voicing an opinion. When he did, his words were carefully weighed, the thought thoroughly digested. He made no spontaneous gestures, and his men were sometimes conscious of a sort of spiritual shell sursounding him, which kept them at a distance. His politeness was unfailing and sincere, to strangers and associates alike. He was soft-spoken, and kind in his thoughts and deeds.

The new captain's first and most important job was to quell the Olguins, who were gloating over what they considered a great triumph. And there was more to it than merely capturing and punishing the slayers of Captain Jones. Texas Ranger honor was at stake. Already certain residents of the district were expressing themselves rather freely about Ranger efficiency, and some of them even were setting their dogs on Ranger horses.

With his usual thoroughness, Hughes went about his task systematically. He sent for "Diamond Dick" St. Leon, the undercover man who had been so valuable to him at Shafter. Pending St. Leon's arrival, the captain and his men made a point of shooting every dog that snapped at their horses' heels. There was a special reason for this, more than a mere point of honor, but Hughes did not enlighten his men.

Rangers patrolled the river bank near San Elizario, and the Olguins knew better than to attempt to cross to Texas at that point. They felt secure on their side of the border, confident that the Rangers would not violate orders from Austin, and come to attack them.

The situation seemed to have reached an impasse, but Captain Hughes went serenely about his duties. In due time, he knew, he would have the information he desired, and then he would take matters into his own hands, and do with them as he saw fit.

Two of the Olguin brothers were in jail in Juarez. Rumors came across the river that they had surrendered voluntarily, and that they were honored guests. At any rate, legal moves to extradite them failed.

After a couple of months, the brothers returned to their old haunts. A big celebration was held to welcome them home. Outlaws from miles around were present. The celebration ended in a drunken brawl, and Antonio Olguin was killed by a dark-skinned stranger, wearing a huge, gold-trimmed sombrero.

Captain Hughes got first-hand information about the death. He heard all the details from a dark-skinned stranger, when he kept a rendezvous with him on the river bank.

A few more weeks passed. Then the Olguin stalwarts were terrified, one morning, to find the body of Pedro Olguin, another of the three brothers, swinging at the end of a rope not far from Tres Jacales.

There was gossip that the dark-skinned stranger with the huge, gold-trimmed sombrero, had been seen in the neighborhood. It suddenly dawned upon the remaining Olguins that certain things were afoot. Jesus Maria Olguin hastily packed a few belongings, and fled into the deep interior, where he reputedly lived out his days in a village south of Mexico City, not daring to return to the border even for a brief visit.

Captain Hughes heard about his flight, and about the death of Pedro, at the same secret meeting place on the banks of the river. That same night, his undercover man handed him a list containing eighteen names—the names of the eighteen men who had participated in the ambush that day when Captain Jones was slain. This was what Hughes had been waiting for, and he hastened back to his Ysleta camp, to launch the plans he had been mulling over for days.

There was a bustle of activities around the camp the next evening, most of it inside the cabins. The Rangers were seeing to their guns, cleaning and oiling them for heavy duty. After midnight, when the streets were deserted, they saddled their horses, and slipped away singly and by pairs, to meet near San Elizario.

At dawn the next morning there was staged the first of a series of raids which made Captain Hughes and his men the most talked about, and praised, persons in the border country. Using the same scheme which had worked so successfully while he was guarding silver bullion shipments, he led his men quietly across the plains, with riders on each flank and one in front, to pick up sentries or stragglers who might race ahead of them to spread an alarm.

Each man had his orders. When they reached the outskirts of the particular settlement in which the wanted men lived, they charged as fast as their mounts would carry them. Two officers dropped off at the first cabin, two at the second, and so on until every shack was covered, and two men had ridden through the settlement to block any possible retreat. Then the men at each cabin went into action.

"Texas Rangers—open up!"

If there was no response inside, the officers at the front door kicked it open and entered with weapons handy to fire quickly at the first sign of resistance.

Captain Hughes usually had information as to the occupants of one particular cabin, and he always picked that cabin to enter himself. More often than not he had to shoot his way both in and out, but he always got his man.

Three names were checked off the list after the first raid. All were taken alive, and eventually all were hanged. There were similar raids two or three dawns in succession, and then sometimes not another for a week or more. Frightened men changed their places of abode, or hid in the hills, but nothing could save them. At the end of about six weeks, every one of the eighteen names had been checked off the list, and every one of the eighteen either died resisting arrest, or was convicted in the courts. This was a great accomplishment for the new captain. A less thorough commander, perhaps, would not have been as successful.

It was during these raids that his men saw the value of the order to shoot all dogs that snapped at their horses' heels. A horse once bitten will always shy at the approach of a dog. The Ranger horses were not bitten, and therefore did not shy to spoil the timing when the packs of dogs around the settlements came yapping at them.

This clean-up completely routed the Olguin gang, and Hughes was now the undisputed

Boss of the Border. Many citizens, especially foreigners and the outlaw elements, doffed their hats and walked around him in circles when they met him on the streets. Officials at Austin blessed the day he was first commissioned.

As a reward for his brilliant undercover work, Captain Hughes made Diamond Dick St. Leon a full-time Ranger. When the Frenchman appeared at Company D camp to be reinstated, he still wore traces of the dye he had used to disguise himself.

Ernest St. Leon was an expert frontiersman, a fearless officer, and one of the most capable undercover men ever enlisted in the Ranger force. He was reared in San Antonio, the son of a refugee French official, and at an early age abandoned the study of law to enlist in the United States cavalry. He fought in several battles with warring tribes of Indians, and won rapid promotion.

As top-sergeant of his army company, he relied upon the friendship and admiration of his men, rather than sharp words, to keep discipline. He was successful because the men knew that their best interests came first with him. On one occasion he allowed himself to be stripped of his highly-prized chevrons before he would divulge the identity of a private implicated in a trivial misdemeanor. On another day he rode out from camp alone and calmly shot to death three Indians who had assassinated one of his men.

St. Leon, who was nick-named because of

his penchant for wearing large diamonds, became a Company D Ranger under Colonel Baylor immediately after he completed his cavalry enlistment, but his army habits could not be countenanced in the state service. He was discharged for drinking while on duty. After Hughes reinstated him, he held an affection for the captain which amounted almost to idolatry. One day the captain admired a silvertrimmed saddle he had purchased, and the generous Frenchman immediately pulled it from his pony's back and insisted that Hughes accept it as a gift.

But Diamond Dick, like many frontiersmen, was a changed man when he was drinking, and alcohol finally caused his downfall. He served Hughes faithfully for a year and a half, and then was shot to death one night in an ugly saloon brawl.

St. Leon and a deputized citizen had arrested three tough cowboys for a minor offense, and then the officer had decided to release them. To demonstrate that there were no ill-feelings, all went together to a saloon. One round of drinks led to another, and soon the shooting began. The deputized civilian was killed instantly, and the Ranger died from his wounds the following day.

CHAPTER VIII

CAPTAIN HUGHES WAS
fortunate in inheriting a roster of fine, capable
officers when he assumed command of Company D. One of the top men was Private
Thalis T. Cook, a tall, dark complexioned,
dangerous looking young fighter whose fierce
countenance frightened bad-men and belied the
fact that he was a bible student and church
worker.

Cook was a dead-eye shot with either Colt or Winchester. He and Hughes were riding together one day when they paused at the top of a hill to watch a pair of coyotes chasing a jack-rabbit. The wily, wolf-like animals took turns in wearing down their prey. One ran the rabbit in a wide circle and then dropped out to let the other continue.

The chase ended on the top of a railroad embankment possibly two-hundred yards from where the officers were sitting on their ponies. As one of the coyotes closed in, Cook raised his Winchester and dropped the animal with a well-placed shot. Captain Hughes fired a few moments later, and got the jack-rabbit.

One of the least told but thoroughly characteristic stories about Private Cook centers around his experiences in connection with his search for Fin Gilliland, a cowboy wanted for the murder of H. H. Poe, a prominent West Texas cattleman.

Private Jim Putman, who accompanied Cook on the scout, had once seen Gilliland, and thought he might recognize him if they came face to face. For this reason, Putman rode ahead on the trail and Cook followed, behind a pack burro. In a small canyon about fifteen miles northwest of Marathon they encountered a lone rider. Putman bowed pleasantly, but Cook eyed the stranger with suspicion. He had pulled off the trail to pass on the left, instead of the right, leaving his pistol hand closest to the officers. This was an advantage usually sought by gunmen; they could use their six-shooters without wheeling their mounts or twisting in their saddles.

Suddenly Cook saw that the stranger was carrying his .45 in his hand, keeping it hidden in the fold of a jacket strapped to his saddle horn. The Ranger turned his pony and started to identify himself as an officer. The man jerked up the weapon and fired once, the bullet knocking Cook from his saddle. Then the stranger spurred his mount, and started away.

"Shoot his horse!" Cook shouted.

Putman quickly raised his Winchester and dropped the animal. The stranger crawled behind the dead beast, and the fight was on. Cook and Putman found shelter behind a rock and fired several volleys before they realized that their opponent was not using his weapons. Several minutes passed. Cook had been shot through the leg, and the wound was painful.

"We can't wait here all day," Cook finally told his companion. "Cover him with your rifle and if he raises his head, let him have it. I'll go out and see if he's had enough."

Using his rifle as a crutch, Cook hobbled toward the enemy. A .45 bullet had found its mark squarely between the stranger's eyes. Papers in his pockets proved that he was Fin Gilliland.

Considerable time elapsed before the Ranger could get medical attention for the wound in his knee. The doctor was pessimistic. "Your leg

will be stiff—you may not be able to use it
much.''

Cook nodded. ''All right, Doc,'' he said.
''Bend it a little and wire it up crooked so I can
ride.''

The Ranger always limped after that, but
the injury in no way interfered with his efficiency as an officer. He fought beside Captain
Hughes in many engagements with outlaws,
and earned a special citation for merit by his
role in one of the most dangerous encounters
in the captain's long list of successes against the
worst criminals in the border country.

Company D was in camp at Ysleta in September, 1896, when Hughes received an urgent
message from a Division Superintendent of the
G., H. & S. A. railroad, stating that a gang of
outlaws was planning to rob a payroll train.
The tip had come from Captain Jim Gillett,
now a prosperous rancher near Marfa. Although he was no longer an officer, Gillett had
led an unsuccessful search for the gang, and had
uncovered information which indicated that
the outlaw camp was located near the little
town of Altuda.

Captain Hughes put three horses and a pack
mule aboard a baggage car. The next morning
he and Cook, and Ranger Private R. E. Bryant
who, as a deputy sheriff, had been present at
the death of Captain Jones, unloaded at Alpine. A bitter, cold rain was falling, but they
mounted their horses and set out immediately.
Deputy Sheriff Jim Pool of Presidio County;

a cowboy named Combs, and Jim Stroud, a rancher who had lost a fine stallion to the thieves, rode with them.

Stroud, also an expert trailer, aided Hughes, and despite the blinding rain they finally found where a small herd of horses and steers had moved across the range, and identified the tracks as having been left by the rustlers. Soaked to the skin and thoroughly miserable, the officers followed the trail all that day, and by noon the next found the spot where the desperadoes had camped overnight.

There were no signs of flour or other provisions at the camp site, other than the carcass of a deer, and Hughes wisely concluded that the outlaws might raid a nearby ranch home, to replenish their scant supplies. With that thought in mind, the officers hastened to the McCutcheon brothers ranch, half expecting to find the buildings in ruins. But the criminals had not been there. As Hughes surveyed the surrounding territory he realized that the men he sought probably were hiding in the rolling mountains a few miles away, and that firing from the heights, they would have the advantage when the fight started.

If the Ranger party with the little pack mule crossed the open range, it could be seen for miles and its members easily identified as officers. Therefore, Hughes sent out his Rangers individually or in pairs, in company with McCutcheon cowboys, hoping that if they were seen by the outlaws, they might be identified merely as cowboys searching for stray stock.

Ranger Cook rode with Jim Stroud and Beau McCutcheon, the latter one of the owners of the ranch. As they cut across a pasture close to the foot of the hills, they came across the trail again. They followed it up a little canyon. Suddenly, from the hill above, came a command.

"Stop there—stay where you are!"

Cook knew instantly that they were close to the gang's camp, but he pretended ignorance. "Why?" he demanded.

The voice from the hilltop cursed. "There's seven rifles pointed at you—turn around and get out of here or we'll let you have it!"

The Ranger stood his ground. "That's not a funny joke," he bantered. "Come down here, and get acquainted."

There were more curses on the hilltop. Then a bullet struck dirt in front of his pony.

The officer had a rifle in his scabbard, but his two companions were armed only with pistols, and pistols would be useless in that fight.

"Go back and get the captain," he instructed in an undertone. "I'll hold 'em here."

As McCutcheon and Stroud turned and spurred their mounts, Cook dove to the ground, rifle in hand, and took shelter behind a rock. The two ranchers heard rifle shots as they raced across the range.

Captain Hughes also heard the shooting, and saw the two horsemen streaking across the range. He and Combs had been searching in another direction. They wheeled, and intercepted the pair.

"They're on that hill!" Stroud shouted, twisting in his saddle to point to the rear. "Cook's trying to hold them until you get there!"

Hughes was extremely fond of the Ranger, and harrowing thoughts ran through his mind. The firing had ceased. Did it mean that the outlaws had killed or wounded the private?

The captain headed his horse toward the hill, which stood up about two hundred feet above the surrounding plain. Combs rode with him. Stroud and McCutcheon quickly got rifles and followed with Deputy Sheriff Pool and several cowboys.

As the captain approached the outlaw's retreat, he could see Cook's horse, but nothing of the Ranger. If his young private lay dead, Hughes vowed he would charge straight up the hill alone, and clean out the robber's nest singlehandedly.

Without slowing his mount, he pulled his rifle from the saddle scabbard and made certain it was ready for use. As he drew nearer, a smile crossed his face. Ranger Cook, crouched behind a large sized rock at the foot of the hill, was waving him a cheerful greeting. Then he motioned to his superior to stay back. The latter knew there must be a special reason for this, and quickly reined in his pony.

He was out of reasonable rifle range from the

hill, and he kept his saddle, eagerly waiting for developments. Suddenly Cook's beautiful roan pony, which had been standing patiently several feet from his master's hiding place, tossed his head, trotted over to the rock, and nudged the young Ranger with his nose. Hughes realized what had happened. Cook, who had trained the animal to come to him in answer to a peculiar low whistle, must have signalled the pony.

A moment later, Cook slipped his rifle into its scabbard, then grasped the saddlehorn with both hands. The fleet animal leaped away like a racing greyhound. Instead of swinging into the saddle, the young Ranger hooked a leg over his mount's back, and hugged its side. The horse made a flying target for the men on the hill, but the rider was scarcely visible to them. They held their fire and the officer rode safely out of range. Pulling himself into the saddle, he galloped up to his commander, grinned and saluted.

"They're still up there, Captain—let's go after them!"

Hughes nodded. "We will—but let's wait until the others get here. We don't want them to escape down the other side of the hill."

While they waited, Cook pointed out the little clump of bushes and rocks from which the gun-fire had been directed at him. It would be a dangerous fortress to storm, the officers knew, but they spent little time discussing it. Instead, they picked out rocks and gullies on the rough hillside which they calculated would give them protection.

Presently the other members of the posse rode up, and Captain Hughes split them into two groups. "You, Pool," he ordered, "take your men around on the left side, and the rest of you go around the right. Don't let any of these outlaws get through you."

The men nodded, and rode off on their assignments. Hughes and Cook galloped their ponies straight toward the enemy's stronghold. Combs, who had been at Hughes' side all afternoon, rode with them.

This show of nerve may have awed the robbers, or perhaps they had decided to save their ammunition for use at close quarters. At any rate, the three fearless men rode beyond Cook's former shelter, and a short distance up the hill, before they were finally fired upon. With the crack of the first rifle, they leaped from their horses and dodged behind rocks. At a signal from Hughes, they returned the fire, as fast as they could.

The battle was on. With the captain leading the way, the three men dodged from shelter to shelter, each move bringing them a little closer to the rock fortress. From the number of shots sent in their direction, Hughes judged that they were facing at least three men, possibly several more. But for every bullet from the hilltop, the officers sent two in return.

Minutes passed. The captain glanced behind him and was amazed to see a fourth man in his little group. He was a youthful health-seeker, who had been staying at the McCutcheon ranch. He had tagged along although armed only with a pistol.

Suddenly Combs stopped firing. His hands flew to the side of his head.

Hughes leaned toward him. "What's the matter?"

The cowboy's hands were wet. "I'm hit," he said. The captain quickly examined the wound. "Just nicked your ear—come on, you aren't hurt."

Combs picked up his rifle and began firing again.

More minutes passed. The officers were almost upon the fortress now. They could hear groans from behind the rocks. At least one of the robbers was hit, but bullets were still coming.

Were the robbers ready to quit? "You'd better surrender!" Hughes yelled.

There was no reply, but the firing ceased on the hill.

"I've got enough!" one of the desperadoes finally shouted.

"Come out with your hands up!" the captain advised.

The officers held their fire. Presently a man walked toward them, hands shoulder high. He had no weapons in sight. Hughes and Cook closed in.

The outlaw strode a few paces, then dodged, and reached in back of him. His hand came out with a pistol which he had tucked inside his belt at the back. He fired at the officers, but Hughes and Cook had fired first. His bullet went wild, and he fell to the ground.

At that instant there were gun-shots at the back of the hill. The officers ran forward in time to see Deputy Sheriff Pool and his men firing at a horseman who was riding away as fast as his pony would travel. The officers were chasing him, but were being outdistanced.

Two of the robbers had died in the fight. They were Jude and Arthur Friar, brothers. Combs was the only posseman hit, and his wound was slight.

After the stolen stock had been returned to its rightful owners, Captain Hughes assigned Cook to run down the robber who had escaped. When the Ranger finally cornered him, he threw down his weapons and surrendered without firing a shot. He was sentenced to a long term in prison.

The young health seeker who had been in the thick of the fight was Arthur McMasters. Before the battle had ended, he had armed himself with a rifle dropped by one of the dead men. In his report to Austin, Captain Hughes made special mention of McMaster's bravery.

The captain was away from his Ysleta camp about a week on this expedition, and in that short time many duties had piled up. He was widely acclaimed in state newspapers, but he had little time, or inclination, to read his press notices. A clipping from a Pecos newspaper, however, was saved by one of his men. It read, in part:

". . . When Captain Hughes heads a party of officers, somebody is going to get caught or killed. A braver or cooler officer has never been commissioned."

CHAPTER IX

As Captain and Boss
of the Border, it was Hughes' duty to send details of men wherever they were needed. When
the assignments were especially dangerous, he
led them himself. His days were filled with active duties, and his nights with keeping the company records, but once a year he managed a
leave to make his quiet pilgrimage to the grave

of his beloved Elizabeth Todd. This was one
mission he never neglected. And neither did he
ever neglect making inquiries whenever possible
as to the whereabouts of Geronimo Parra, the
murderer of Sergeant Fusselman.

Lists of wanted criminals were published
yearly by the Texas Adjutant General's office
and when no more pressing duties were at hand,
Rangers were required to scout through the bad-
lands along the border in search of any of the
fugitives they might run across in the outlaw
hide-outs. Rarely a month passed that Hughes
did not lead his men in one or more expeditions
of this nature.

Ben Williams, a deputy under Sheriff Martin
Lohman, of Las Cruces, New Mexico, about
forty miles north of El Paso, frequently rode
with Company D Rangers, for outlaws from
his county usually fled to the border whenever
they hoped to avoid arrest.

Captain Hughes and Williams set out alone
one day on a scout along the Rio Grande near
Fort Hancock, and as their ponies jogged along
the trail they overtook two horsemen who,
upon seeing them, spurred their mounts and
tried to escape through the Manzanita bench.
The officers gave chase and quickly rounded up
the pair. Hughes did not recognize either as being wanted for crimes in Texas, but one, who
had given his name as Roberto, was claimed by
Williams for a robbery in Las Cruces. The
man was taken there, tried and convicted, and

sentenced to a long term in the New Mexico prison.

A few weeks later, Captain Hughes was saddened to learn that Deputy Williams had suffered critical wounds in a gun-fight with an outlaw. Williams had gone to an adobe house in Las Cruces to arrest the man when suddenly the latter had opened fire. The officer was hit in the shoulder but he shot his way into the house and dragged out his prisoner. The gunman gave his name as Juan Flores, and was sentenced to the prison at Santa Fé.

Many border officers were wounded in the line of duty, and Hughes quickly forgot the incident. Then one day came the tip for which he had long waited. According to an informant, Juan Flores was in reality Geronimo Parra. And Roberto, the man Hughes and Williams had captured in the Manzanita, had been a member of the robber gang led by Parra on that day when Sergeant Fusselman was slain.

Hughes eagerly investigated the tip, verified it, and wired Governor Charles Culberson, at Austin, asking him to make formal request for custody of Parra. The Governor immediately dispatched papers to Santa Fé,̇ but the murderer had powerful friends in New Mexico territory. The authorities flatly refused to turn either him or Roberto over to anyone, regardless of the charges against them.

Hughes already had made plans to go after the prisoners and he was greatly disappointed. But he would get Parra some day. Several years already had passed since he had vowed to capture the murderer, dead or alive, and he could wait a while longer if necessary.

Weeks passed and then one day the captain had a distinguished caller at the Ranger camp. The visitor was the renowned Pat Garrett, the famous peace officer who had killed Billy the Kid. Since Garrett had retired to his ranch near Uvalde, Texas, outlawry had gotten out of hand in Las Cruces, and the New Mexico authorities had begged him to come there and restore order. He had accepted the assignment, and had stopped to visit his old friend, Captain Hughes, en route to Las Cruces.

The men had a fine visit, and before Garrett left, his host made him a proposition.

"Pat," he said, "you'll be one man in New Mexico whom the authorities won't refuse anything. I want Geronimo Parra—you know that. He's in prison over there. Get him for me, will you?"

Garrett grinned. "For an old friend—yes."

Hughes explained what powerful influences the Mexican seemed to have at his command. Pat, however, was certain that he could successfully combat them. He departed promising to send Hughes early word when to come for the prisoner. But a month passed, and another, and no word. The Ranger grew discouraged again. Then, finally, he received a letter from his old friend.

"I want a man named Pat Agnew, who is running loose somewhere in Texas," Garrett wrote. "He's six feet three, weighs two hundred pounds. He carries two guns, and he's quick with them. Get him for me and I'll give you Parra."

Bringing Parra to justice was a personal matter with the captain, so he determined to handle the entire matter himself. But where could he start searching for Agnew? He checked with his informers, and got little information about the criminal. One knew him, and said that he had lost the little finger off his left hand in a knife fight. This was an identifying mark Hughes was glad to get. Another man told him that he believed Agnew had friends who resided in the Big Bend.

Hughes pounced onto this lead. He knew every inch of the Big Bend country, and knew exactly how to put out lines to catch outlaws in that territory. He immediately set out from his Ysleta camp, and a few days later arrived at the isolated little shack of an Indian half-breed, deep in the Big Bend wilds.

The captain quickly located the Indian, and called him to one side, out of hearing of members of his family. "Frank, I'm looking for Pat Agnew," the Ranger began. "You know him—he's a big man, and he doesn't have a little finger on his left hand."

Frank shrugged. "I don't see much—you know that, Captain," he said.

Hughes' face grew grim. "Frank, I think you and I had better take a little ride into Del Rio. I want to take your picture, and write some letters. Maybe I can find out where you came from."

The man shifted uneasily, and Hughes knew he had scored a point. "You'd better saddle up," he continued.

"I remember now," Frank told him hastily. "The big man was here, maybe five, six months ago. Said he was going to Carrizo."

Frank swore that he was not lying. Hughes galloped away. At Carrizo he learned that Agnew had been there, but had left again, doubling back toward the Pecos country. Hughes rode after him, making inquiries at every town and settlement he passed.

He lived for days and weeks in the saddle, subsisting on bread and beans. He rode the shoes off his mounts and reshod on the trail. He was completely out of touch with his camp, and state affairs. He realized that there must be many matters piling up at the camp, waiting for his personal attention, but he could not turn back. He had vowed to get Geronimo Parra, and if this was the way it had to be done, he would do it this way.

After several weeks of patient detective work, and hundreds of miles of hard riding, he finally located Agnew, working at a small ranch not far from the border. He rode there, as fast as he could. The rancher came out to greet him.

"Is there a man named Agnew working here?" he asked.

The rancher nodded. "Why yes."

At that moment a tall, heavy set man came

around the corner of the cabin. He had his
hands on the butts of two pistols in their holsters, but he did not draw. The Ranger recognized him instantly. "I'm Captain Hughes,"
he announced. "I want you."

The criminal stood motionless. Hughes
watched him closely expecting him to draw.
Both men were tense, and ready.

"Is it right?" the startled rancher demanded
of his cowboy.

The latter hesitated. "Guess it is," he finally
replied. He surrendered his weapons meekly,
and Hughes took him to El Paso, where he sent
a telegram to Pat Garrett.

"Holding Agnew here. When do I get
Parra?"

Garrett hastened to El Paso. He was delight-
ed. He took the prisoner to Las Cruces, and
then he and Captain Hughes went to Santa Fé.

The Territorial Governor received them
warmly, but when Garrett explained their
mission, he frowned. "I'm afraid I can't let you
have him," he said. "Parra has a long sentence
to serve here in New Mexico."

Garrett flushed. "All right, then, I'm
through—through with New Mexico."

The Governor leaped up. "Wait! Don't be
hasty, Pat!"

"Hasty?" Garrett shouted. "I promised
John Hughes he could have Parra. Since when
have I failed to keep my promises?"

The men argued, and finally Pat was the

victor. He was given custody of Parra and at the border turned him over to Captain Hughes.

It was a proud day for the captain when he locked the outlaw in the El Paso jail. He attended the trial, and was present when the prisoner was found guilty of the Fusselman murder. He was also present, months later, when the Mexican was hanged for the crime. Although it had taken him nine years, he had finally avenged the death of his friend and brother Ranger.

By the time Pat Garrett had finally restored order in Las Cruces, he had grown to like the town. He disposed of his Texas holdings and settled down there to spend the rest of his days. He had won many gun-fights in his lifetime, but on the last day of February, 1908, he died beside a trail near Las Cruces, with a bullet through the heart.

Notarized statements on file in the library of the old Governors' Palace, at Santa Fé, give an account of the shooting as told by a purported eye-witness. According to these papers, Garrett argued over the size of a goat herd belonging to a tenant on his land, and this tenant beat him to the draw.

Captain Hughes never agreed with this version of his old friend's death. He made no formal investigation at the time, but obtained much information about the affair from unimpeachable sources. Hughes believed that Garrett was "put on the spot" and assassinated by a professional killer, not the rancher, who had been hired to do the job by one of Pat's political enemies.

In the first place, the county coroner found the fly of the dead man's trousers unbuttoned. It was established that Garrett had been standing in privacy beside a mesquite bush when he was shot. To Hughes' mind, this disproved the claim that the experienced old gun-fighter could have been engaged in an argument when the fatal shot was fired. Moreover, no ordinary rancher would have been capable of getting out his firearms and using them ahead of Garrett, had the latter been given any kind of a chance.

Hughes was of the opinion that if Jim Miller, notorious Texas gunman, did not actually fire the fatal shot, he was close at hand when Garrett breathed his last.

Pat was an unusually tall man, and when it came time to bury him, the undertaker discovered that he had no casket long enough to take the body. An urgent message was sent to El Paso, and an undertaker from that city hastened to Las Cruces with a burial box of the required length. Upon his return to El Paso, this undertaker told Captain Hughes that he had seen Jim Miller in Las Cruces, in conversation with a certain man Hughes knew as one of Garrett's enemies. At that time, Miller resided in Fort Worth.

"Killer" Miller murdered many men before he finally was strung up by an infuriated lynch mob, and it was while dealing with him that Captain Hughes became acquainted with John

Wesley Hardin who, with thirty or more notches on his six-shooter, was generally regarded as the most dangerous gun-fighter in the blood-soaked history of the border country.

In the early '90's, one Bud Frazer was sheriff at Pecos in Reeves County, and hired Jim Miller as a deputy when the latter arrived in Pecos from his home in Central Texas. Miller was about twenty-two at the time, and had left home after killing a brother-in-law. Frazer assigned the young deputy to escort a prisoner to Fort Stockton one day, and came in for considerable criticism when Miller killed the man, claiming that he had tried to escape.

Some months later, cattlemen in Reeves County began losing stock, and it was discovered that the animals were being driven south across the border. Miller was frequently absent from his home for long periods and Frazer, suspecting he knew something about the thefts, had a talk with him. A couple of weeks later, Captain Hughes received a message which sent him and a couple of Rangers to Pecos, posthaste. They arrested Miller and three others on charges of conspiracy to kill the sheriff. A man who claimed he had been invited to accompany the assassin had revealed the alleged plot to Frazer.

Miller and one associate were indicted, and tried at El Paso. They were cleared. The informer who had implicated them was found murdered in New Mexico, and a short time later Frazer and Miller came face to face on a

Pecos street. Frazer fired first with his six-shooter, and his bullet hit his opponent in the right arm. Some weeks later they met again, Frazer armed with a rifle and Miller a double-barreled shotgun. Again Miller was pinked.

In the meantime, there had been an election in Reeves County, and Frazer had been ousted from office. The new sheriff stepped in after this second duel and arrested Frazer. He was tried in El Paso, and the jury could not reach agreement. A second trial was called at Colorado City, and feeling was so intense between the principals that Captain Hughes was present to keep the peace.

John Wesley Hardin appeared at this second trial, seeking to aid Miller, whose wife was Hardin's cousin. As a boy during "reconstruction," the gun-fighter had killed a half dozen Negro policemen one afternoon. Later he was arrested and sentenced to serve 15 years in the Texas prison, studied law in his cell, and upon release was admitted to the bar.

It was predicted that, with Hardin present in Colorado City, there would be gun-play, but when it was seen that Captain Hughes was also among those in attendance, this opinion changed. No disorder of any kind developed, even when the jury returned a verdict acquitting Frazer.

The feud remained at a standstill for several weeks after the trial. At length Frazer went to the town of Toyah to pay a political debt by aiding a friend's campaign for a county office.

He was sitting in a saloon playing cards when Miller stepped through a rear door and emptied a shotgun into his back. Frazer died instantly.

Miller was indicted but it was several months before his trial was called. He returned to Pecos and became proprietor of a hotel there. He joined a church, contributed generously to charities, and otherwise courted supporters among the town's better citizens. When the case against him was moved to the court at Eastland, a village near Fort Worth, he moved there and transferred his church membership. At his first trial the jury could not agree, and at the second he was acquitted.

Miller remained in the vicinity of Fort Worth, but fell upon bad times. He moved to the Panhandle, and finally to Oklahoma where he and three companions were jailed at Ada, charged with a brutal murder. A mob stormed the jail, dragged him and his companions out, and hanged all four of them.

John Wesley Hardin lost interest in his kinsman's troubles after the Colorado City trial. He remained in El Paso, and became involved in one or two unpleasant scandals. His law practice, what there was of it, fell off and finally he began frequenting the city's saloons and resorts.

Hardin paid no attention to the warnings of his supporters that one or another of the tough gun-fighters in the Southwest might take an unfair advantage in winning the distinction of beating him to the draw. He believed he could out-shoot anyone he faced.

His name came into the conversation one day while Captain Hughes and a group of officers were on a scout along the Rio Grande. The sheriff from Fort Davis was riding beside Hughes. "They say Wes Hardin is cutting capers in El Paso," the officer commented. "What's going to happen, Captain?"

"Why, someone will kill him," Hughes replied.

"Who?"

"See that man in the blue britches over there?" Hughes pointed to a member of the posse. "He might do it."

The man in the blue britches was George Scarborough, a Deputy U. S. Marshal from El Paso. Later that same day the possemen learned that the bandits they were seeking were a hundred miles ahead of them, and Hughes and Scarborough boarded a train, to attempt to head them off. The conductor recognized them when he checked their passes.

"Have you heard the news in El Paso?" he asked.

"What news?" Scarborough demanded.

"Why, Wes Hardin was killed."

Scarborough grumbled. "Who did it?"

"John Selman."

The Deputy Marshal shook his head. "I'll bet he shot him in the back."

He was correct. Selman, the City Marshal who had killed Bass Outlaw and many another

gunman, argued with Hardin over an arrest
made by Selman's son, a city police officer. A
gun-fight was inevitable. Hardin was standing
at the bar in a saloon when the Marshal entered,
and he must have seen the first quick movement through the back-bar mirror when Selman whipped out his pistol and put a bullet in
the back of Hardin's head.

The jealousies which frequently bedeviled
old-time peace officers kept Selman and Scarborough at odds after that, and their relations
soon reached a climax in a heated exchange of
words. They walked about the city eyeing one
another suspiciously for a few days, then met
in a saloon one night, and stepped into the rear
courtyard to have it out. Scarborough fired
first; Selman died. And less than a year later,
Scarborough also lay dead from bullet wounds.
He was ambushed by a gang of outlaws he was
trailing in New Mexico.

Captain Hughes remembered both men as
fearless officers. When official business took
him to El Paso, he frequently accepted Scarborough's invitation to accompany him to din-
ner. After the meal in the comfortable Scarborough home, the deputy marshal's daughters
usually played hymns on the organ, and their
father led the singing.

CHAPTER X

CAPTAIN HUGHES MAIN-
tained strict standards for his Company D
Rangers. A widely syndicated newspaper article once stated that he enlisted only teetotalers
who were church members and non-smokers.
This was not true, but he did seek men whose
reputations were beyond reproach, and he demanded that they be polite and gentlemanly at
all times. They were officers of the state of

Texas, he frequently reminded them, and as such they must conduct themselves in a way to do honor to a great people.

He attached special importance to their qualifications as peace officers, and recruited only those capable of capturing outlaws by their brains as well as by their bullets and brawn. A good detective, or a good fighter, was not enough—he wanted only men who were both. He was an excellent investigator himself, and required assistants who were the same, for frequently Austin officials detailed him to special assignments which did not entail fighting outlaws.

Governor O. B. Colquitt once put Hughes on the trail of a desperate murderer known as Joe Dean and before the case was finally closed, it called for talents seldom expected in a gun-slinging border Ranger. Dean, under a fifty-year sentence, had escaped from a Texas prison farm. The captain trailed him to New Orleans, and learned that he had boarded a boat for Spanish Honduras.

Months later the fugitive returned, and began operating a saloon in Juarez. Hughes learned about it, and learned also that the criminal had fallen in love with a beautiful señorita named Chapita. He had brought his wife and children to Juarez, and the Mexican girl resided in the same house with them.

Dean was a dangerous man when he was drinking, and the captain was confident that, soon or late, he would become embroiled with the Mexican authorities. It came sooner than the Ranger expected. The saloon-keeper and another man were arrested by Juarez police, charged with shooting at a Mexican citizen in an effort to steal his automobile. They were held in the Juarez jail.

Captain Hughes immediately communicated with Governor Colquitt, and the latter prepared extradition papers, requesting the Mexican authorities to turn the prisoner over to Texas officers. There was considerable delay in getting the orders approved by the Governor of Chihuahua, and Hughes had the uncomfortable feeling that the Juarez police might release the fugitive. So finally he took the matter into his own hands.

He had informers on both sides of the river, and through one of these had word carried to the Mexican girl, Chapita, to the effect that Dean was to be extradited the following morning, and since he was facing a long prison sentence in Texas, he would be lost to her forever.

At dusk that evening, the captain laid aside his sombrero and other apparel which might identify him as an officer, and went across the Rio Grande, posing as a visitor seeking an evening's entertainment in the Mexican city. He was accompanied by his informer. They kept a watch on the jail, and about midnight found a hiding place in deep shadows across the street from the dreary building.

By three A. M., Hughes had decided that his scheme had failed. He was about to return to the American side of the river when he saw a girl stealing quietly down the street toward the jail. The informer whispered that she was Chapita. Next, a lone horseman appeared. The girl and the *charro* conversed for a few moments, and the latter rode his mount close to the jail wall, unwound a *riata,* and tossed one end over the wall into the courtyard.

Hughes strained his eyes to watch every movement. Presently a belfry clock chimed three, and he realized that this might be a pre-arranged signal. It was. Soon there was a tug on the *riata,* and the *charro* whipped his horse. A man was clinging to the end of the rope, and when his head and shoulders appeared over the wall, Hughes recognized him as Dean. The prisoner jumped off the wall—and then writhed on the ground. He had injured his leg in the leap.

Hughes had given his informer careful instructions. Now he nudged him, and the Mexican ran up to Chapita, who was kneeling beside the injured man. He began speaking rapidly in her native tongue. He had seen the escape, he told the girl, and she had his fullest sympathy. "But, quick—you must get him away before the guards shoot," he exclaimed. "It will not be safe in Mexico—you must take him across the Rio Grande." He added a strongly worded admonition that the injury should be treated immediately by an American doctor.

The girl and Dean heeded the advice, and the

informer ran to bring them a taxi-cab. Captain Hughes slipped away then, got into another taxi he had waiting, and by taking a short-cut reached the river bridge first. When Joe Dean stepped foot on United States soil, the captain placed him under arrest, and a few days later returned him to the custody of the prison authorities.

Hughes was glad that the affair was over. Acting, in a sense, as an *agent provocateur* had been distasteful to him, but Dean was a dangerous criminal and any trick that would lead to his recapture and imprisonment was justifiable.

Behind bars again, the murderer wrote an impassioned appeal to the Governor, requesting "a few days furlough" during which he might get custody of his children from his wife, and arrange for their future care. Governor Colquitt, a kind, just man, had no intention of allowing the furlough of such a dangerous character, but he forwarded the letter to Captain Hughes with a request that the Ranger investigate further, with the view of placing the Dean youngsters in an orphanage if the mother was not a proper guardian.

By this time Mrs. Dean had disappeared from the vicinity of El Paso, and acquaintances thought she had moved to Arizona. Hughes checked railroad ticket offices and draymen, and finally traced her, instead, to a South Texas community. In the meantime, he had visited a number of small hotels and rooming houses, and had prevailed upon the managers to give him affidavits which set forth that the woman did not provide the children with proper moral surroundings.

The Governor ordered him to follow up the matter, so the captain traveled to South Texas, and finally located the woman. She hotly denied the allegations against her, and vowed that she would never surrender her children to anyone. Hughes was in a quandary. Accusing a woman of bad morals was difficult enough, but just how should he, a gun-fighting border Ranger, go about tearing two babies from their mother's arms?

He could have sought the aid of county officers who were more experienced in handling juvenile cases, but the Governor's orders in his pocket assigned him to deliver the youngsters to the orphanage. He mopped his brow and began talking, as rapidly and as convincingly as he knew how. He suggested to the mother that she might be glad to escape the financial burden and pointed out in glowing terms that the youngsters would have excellent care. Then he swung into the benefits any youngsters could expect in being the wards of the great state of Texas, with all its vast resources.

He must have been convincing, for the young woman finally agreed to accompany him to the office of the Probate Judge. And upon their arrival, she capitulated and signed the necessary papers. An hour later she delivered the babies to the railroad station and, blushing furiously, Captain Hughes carried them aboard a train.

There is no limit to what Texas asks of her Rangers! Before that short journey was over, the bachelor captain had been forced to master the intricacies of triangular panties, but they were two smiling, happy young-ones that he turned over to the orphanage officials. Eyes twinkling, he demanded and got a receipt for them, which he forwarded to Austin. The Governor was solemnly appreciative:

"I beg to thank you sincerely for the discreet and good manner in which you have handled this entire matter," he wrote the captain.

Another special assignment arrived in Hughes' mail one morning early in '96, just as he returned from a scout during which he and two privates had ridden four hundred miles in nine days, and had arrested two rustlers and recovered sixteen stolen horses. He was ordered to set out immediately, and by any means he deemed necessary, prevent Bob Fitzsimmons, then a leading contender for the heavyweight boxing championship of the world, from meeting a challenger within the boundaries of Texas.

Fitzsimmons and his handlers were traveling across the state. Hughes followed them into Arkansas, and then returned to his camp, satisfied that he had completed the job. But within a few days the boxer and his party arrived in El Paso, where it was announced that a small group of citizens had posted a purse of $10,000 to be paid the winner of a fight there between Fitzsimmons and Pete Maher, another leading contender for the heavyweight crown.

Captain Hughes got on the job promptly. Singlehandedly, he could have stopped a dozen such fights—everyone knew that—but for some reason, Austin authorities sent every Texas Ranger in the service to El Paso, under command of Adjutant General Mabry. Ranger captains dogged the footsteps of all the principals. The promoters threatened to bring in Bat Masterson, and a gang of gun-fighters from the North, and stage the bout anyway, but they really knew better than to do that.

It was soon apparent to the sportsmen that the fight could not be held in El Paso, and the Governor of Chihuahua blocked plans for holding it across the Rio Grande. As an excuse for delay, it was announced that Maher had developed "acute ophthalmia." With matters at a standstill, the Rangers had little to do. Captain Hughes arrested and jailed a couple of confidence men he apprehended in the act of fleecing a local merchant, and other Rangers quieted a fight between two gamblers. That was the extent of official activity.

Finally both fight camps boarded trains and departed. The Rangers tagged along. At Langtry, Texas, scene of Judge Roy Bean's saloon-courtroom, the fighters disembarked, and went across the Rio Grande into Mexico. The Rangers sat on the Texas bank, and watched proceedings through binoculars. But there wasn't much to see. The fight lasted less than half a round—just long enough for the mighty Fitz to uncork his man-killing punch.

Captain Hughes knew Roy Bean, although it never happened that he had a prisoner in Bean's territory to take before the bar of the saloon-court in Langtry. Sports writers attending this boxing match wrote colorful stories about the eccentric westerner who was such a great admirer of the Jersey Lily, and made him famous in the East.

The captain discovered in later years that Bean was maligned in books, newspapers and movies, although there was some basis of fact for tall stories about him. He made his laughable interpretations of the law to win publicity, to amuse his friends, and sometimes to clear the docket of cases which were likely to remain unsolved.

Some little time after the prize-fight episode, Hughes was confronted with another perplexing problem which called for more than mere fighting ability. Stockmen in the vicinity of Fort Hancock were suffering heavy losses from rustlers. All the evidence pointed squarely to the guilt of a certain rancher in the neighborhood, but none of the stolen stock could be found in his pastures. His herds were growing rapidly, but the brands were untampered, and he could show bills of sale for the new steers.

Hughes and his men weighed the evidence, and were still suspicious. Finally they hit upon what they believed was the correct answer, and the captain and three privates rode away on a scout. They traveled south, and when they reached the vicinity of Crow Flat, about forty miles down the Rio Grande, received the information they were seeking.

A certain man in that locality had recently acquired a new herd of steers. When the Rangers visited his pasture, they identified some of the brands as those of the Fort Hancock stockmen who had reported heavy losses.

The officers might have arrested this man and his helpers, seized the stock, obtained a conviction in court, and considered the whole matter settled. But they made no immediate arrests. Instead, they continued making inquiries until they finally identified the brands they had seen in the Fort Hancock pasture.

Then, simultaneously, they arrested the Crow Flat rancher, and the Fort Hancock suspect. The two had been working together, as the Company D men had suspected. Each rustled animals in his own territory and then they traded the stolen animals, and forged bills of sale, so that each could remain in the clear among his neighbors.

Six of the eight men in the two gangs were convicted, and the remaining two fled to New Mexico. Stockmen at Crow Flat had not known that their herds had been raided until Hughes and his Rangers returned the stolen animals.

The detective work of Company D men also was of great assistance to Hughes in the prominent role he played in the famous "Little Abey" Hummel conspiracy case, in New York City. This was in 1904. It made the captain nationally known and did much to heighten the prestige of the Texas Ranger service.

Abraham H. Hummel was a New York attorney with an amazing record of courtroom success, but in the words of New York's District Attorney Jerome, he had been "for twenty years, a menace to the community." He was accused of bribing jurors, falsifying evidence, and about everything else that was unethical and illegal in his practice. At last District Attorney Jerome obtained evidence that the lawyer had used false affidavits and extorted exorbitant fees in a divorce mixup. He was promptly indicted for conspiracy.

The state's main witness was Charles F. Dodge, who had signed the affidavits Hummel had concocted, and who also was under indictment. Before the case could be brought to trial, Dodge forfeited $10,000 bond and disappeared. A detective from the District Attorney's office traced him to New Orleans, and then into Texas. Hummel boasted of "a million dollar fund" which would guarantee that Dodge was never returned to New York City, and Jerome accepted the challenge. Both sides engaged high-powered Texas attorneys, and the legal battle started.

When it was apparent that Dodge might slip across the border to the security of Mexico, the New York detective contacted Captain Hughes, then in camp at Alice, and Hughes received orders from Austin to stop the witness from leaving the United States. He assigned two of his

crack Company D Rangers to the matter—
Sergeant Tom M. Ross and Private James F.
Harrod. Ross trailed Dodge, and Harrod worked undercover. When the New Yorker accompanied by Hummel's aides, arrived at Alice preparatory to boarding the Mexico City Flier,
Ranger Harrod was acting as night clerk of the
hotel where they stopped.

Harrod reported their movements and con-
versations to Captain Hughes, and several days
later when they slipped aboard a Mexico bound
train, Hughes placed the witness under arrest.
He reported to Austin and received the following telegram:

"Hold C. F. Dodge to await requisition from
Governor of New York. (Signed) S. W. T.
Lanham, Governor."

Hummel's Texas representatives promptly
trained their big guns on the Ranger captain.
An officer from nearby Nueces County arrived
with a writ of *habeas corpus* designed so that
Hummel's agents might get custody of Dodge.
Hughes produced the telegram from the Governor.

"I'm sorry, but I don't find a thing in this
about turning the prisoner over to you," he
said.

He paid no attention to the officer's protest
that he was defying a court order.

When a deputy sheriff from adjacent Bee
County arrived with similar court papers,
Hughes asked him how long it had been that
Bee County was a part of New York.

Finally a federal court judge at Houston sent a United States Marshal to claim the prisoner. Captain Hughes calmly explained that he had his orders, and that he intended to obey them. He held the prisoner and until Governor Lanham rescinded his original notice—well, he would like to see anyone try to take the prisoner away from him.

Some time later, however, and with the Governor's approval, Hughes did take Dodge to federal court in Houston, and the witness was ultimately sent back to New York. Hummel was convicted and sentenced to prison. The captain refused a huge bribe which had been offered him from the "million dollar fund" if he would allow Dodge to escape. Undoubtedly the case would have had a far different ending if a man of less character had been in his position.

Shortly prior to this episode, Company D had been transferred to Alice and the lower Rio Grande Valley from the El Paso region to relieve Company A, under Capt. J. A. Brooks. Sergeant A. Y. Baker, second in command of A company, had become involved in a feud with certain lower valley residents, and the Adjutant General had deemed it expedient to settle the matter by having Hughes take over.

Baker and Private W. E. Roebuck had killed a Mexican when the latter had resisted arrest, and a few days later the two Rangers and a cowboy were ambushed. Roebuck was killed and the sergeant seriously wounded. When it was apparent that the latter would recover, word was passed to Captain Brooks that a certain ranchman, a brother of the slain Mexican, had vowed to try again to dispose of Baker, if and when he returned to duty.

The sergeant looked to his weapons, and when he was able to ride again, went seeking the ranchman. They met and the Ranger drew first. With two members of the Mexican family now dead, other kinsmen vowed revenge and the Adjutant General ordered Company A out of the district to prevent further bloodshed.

Hughes had many friends among the citizens of West Texas, and their sentiments about his leaving that area were expressed in an article in the *El Paso Daily Times*, which read in part:

"He (Hughes) never yet started after a criminal he did not capture or kill. The people in general and the officers in particular of El Paso County will regret to learn that Captain Hughes is to leave them. His many sterling qualities, his fearlessness, devotion to duty and unruffled courtesy under any and all circumstances have endeared him to the people of this country."

The Company D Rangers, hardened to frequent skirmishes with the tough Big Bend outlaws, found time heavy on their hands in the more peaceful surroundings of Alice. Only twice a year—in the early spring when migratory laborers began crossing the Rio Grande to go north for seasonal work, and again in the fall when they returned—was there need for any great amount of the scouting upon which they thrived.

This was not as true, however, in Brownsville and the territory around the mouth of the Rio Grande. Marauding bands of outlaws from across the border made frequent raids upon ranches there, and Hughes and his men often engaged them in gun-fights. After one successful scout, the Rangers returned to Brownsville with a half dozen prisoners, and more than a hundred head of stolen cattle.

Finding the owners of the animals was a difficult problem. The thieves had burned off the brands, and one longhorn looked about the same as another. Hughes guessed that the calves in the herd must have been stolen from milk pens, and finally he hit upon a solution. He instructed the ranchers who had lost stock to bring their children to the corral. They did, and the youngsters recognized most of the calves, and could call them by name. The mothers of the calves could thus be identified, and the mix-up was fairly well untangled.

The Ranger commander was praised for his ingenuity, and highly complimented following another incident which occurred at about the same time. A well-known rancher who resided near Brownsville called at the Ranger camp one night, seeking advice as to what steps he should take in handling a hard-cased cowboy he had recently discharged.

"You say he has threatened to kill you?" Captain Hughes asked.

"That's right—he's boasting that he'll put a bullet through my heart before sundown tomorrow. I'm willing to run my chances on that, but I don't want to kill him unless I have to."

Hughes saddled his pony and accompanied the visitor home. About noon the next day the cowboy appeared in front of the ranch house, six-shooters in holsters strapped to each leg, and shouted for the owner to come out and face him. Hughes instructed the rancher to remain out of sight and, with his ever-present rifle across his arm, stepped suddenly through the door. The cowboy stared at him, hands held rigidly in position for a quick draw.

"What do you want?" Hughes demanded, sternly.

The man did not reply, and the captain walked slowly toward him, ready for action at the first flicker of motion.

"I'm Captain Hughes of the Texas Rangers," he continued, "and I've heard about your big talk."

The cowboy's expression changed and his bluster vanished. He knew the Ranger by reputation. "Yes sir, Captain," he mumbled, backing toward his pony.

Hughes kept advancing. "There isn't going to be any trouble here—get going, and don't ever come back! If you make any more threats —I'll be after you!"

The cowboy nodded vigorously. "Yes sir . . . yes sir . . ." He finally reached his mount, scrambled into the saddle, and rode away as fast as the animal would carry him.

Some days later the ranch owner again visited the Ranger camp. The captain had saved his life, he insisted. He presented Hughes with a beautifully engraved Colt .45 pistol, with the white ivory handle carved to fit the fingers of the captain's left hand. Hughes carried the weapon for many years, and even after his retirement it was never far from his reach.

CHAPTER XI

T HE TEXAS RANGERS were organized as a military force in 1835, during the revolution of Texas against Mexico, but it was not until 1874 that laws were passed creating the Frontier Battalion. This little band of fighters engaged Indians and marauding Mexicans until there were no more battle fronts, and then took over the duties of a police force, stopping feuds, breaking up gangs of rustlers and stage robbers, and killing or capturing murderers.

Governor Joseph D. Sayers discovered, however, that the statutes under which the Rangers functioned did not give them police powers, and on June 1, 1900, he abolished the Frontier Battalion, by reducing it to a skeleton force. A year later, on July 8, 1901, the legislature passed new laws creating a Ranger force of four companies, definitely charged with the responsibility of "protecting the frontier against marauding or thieving parties, and suppressing lawlessness and crime throughout the state."

Captain Hughes had been a Frontier Battalion commander, and he and the three other captains who had won distinction in the battalion were given command of the new force. They were, besides Hughes who was in charge of Company D, Captain Brooks, in command of Company A; Capt. W. J. McDonald, in charge of Company B; and Capt. J. H. Rogers, Company C.

With only this limited force at his command, the Adjutant General was obliged to make frequent shifts in assignments. Company D remained in the valley for several months and then Hughes and his men were transferred back to the El Paso and the Big Bend area, where border fighters were greatly needed. Company B took over at Alice.

Captain "Bill" McDonald, the B company commander, undoubtedly was the most publicized Ranger officer of his day. He had demonstrated his bravery many times, and was a competent as well as a fearless officer. Most of his service was in the more thickly populated interior of the state, where his salty talk made splendid newspaper copy. He was credited with all the accomplishments of his company, sometimes even when one of the privates was more properly entitled to praise, and his fame spread.

In 1906, while Company B was at Alice, colored federal troops at Fort Brown, near Brownsville, ran amuck and shot up the town, killing one citizen and wounding several. Captain McDonald hastened to the fort to make arrests. When he was temporarily thwarted, he defied the whole United States army to keep him from doing his duty. The affair dragged along for weeks and finally ended in a standoff, with the soldiers acquitted but their commanding officers dismissed.

Three months later, on the eve of the November election, rioting broke out in Rio Grande City, and District Judge Stanley Welch was assassinated as he slept in his home. Governor Lanham reached McDonald at Alice, by telephone, and ordered him to hasten to the scene and quell the disturbance.

The captain and Sergeant W. J. McCauley, his nephew, were alone in camp. They set out immediately, accompanied by Crosby Marsden, a citizen volunteer. At Harlingen they were joined by Ranger Sam McKenzie and U. S. Customs Inspector Blaze Delling, an ex-Ranger. They were forced to travel a circuitous route and it was nearly dusk when they dropped off the train at Sam Fordyce and hired a man with a team and wagon to take them the remaining twenty miles.

The officers had received only vague reports as to the extent of the rioting, and could only guess as to what manner of fighting would be required of them. They kept a sharp watch for possible ambush parties lurking beside the desolate trail. At about 8:30 p. m., when they had covered half the distance, they suddenly heard shouting ahead.

Captain McDonald ordered the team driver to pull to the side of the trail, and deployed his men carefully in positions where they could do the most good, should the oncomers start a battle. Presently the Rangers could hear the grinding wheels of some sort of vehicle. Then there were pistol shots, and bullets whistled over their heads. The officers examined their weapons—and waited. Finally a team and hack came over the hill in front of them.

"Texas Rangers—halt for inspection!" Captain McDonald shouted. McKenzie repeated the challenge in Spanish.

Almost simultaneously, there were more shots from the hack.

The battle was a furious one while it lasted. But it was over inside of a minute. None of the Rangers was hit. Four of their opponents were killed outright, one was wounded, and two captured. All were Mexicans. The captain, sitting on the wagon seat beside the driver, was carried from the scene when the team ran away and his rifle jammed. It wasn't until sometime later, when the other run-away was caught, that two of the dead men were discovered inside the hack.

The Rangers took their prisoners into Rio Grande City. They disarmed all men who were carrying weapons openly, and appeared to have the situation well in hand. But there was an undercurrent of unrest which McDonald, unfamiliar with the border people, could not classify. It was among the Mexican residents, and there were more than four times as many of them as there were Americans.

If he was alarmed, he made no mention of it in the crisp report he telegraphed to Austin. But officials at the Adjutant General's office knew that further trouble might be expected at any moment and knew, too, that there was one man who could prevent it, if anyone could. Captain Hughes, away on a scout, was reached by telephone and accompanied by Adjutant General John A. Hulen, set out for Rio Grande City by rail.

At Sam Fordyce they were joined by a group of citizens, and cowboys from the famous King Ranch, who had been ordered to bring fifteen ponies, saddled and equipped, for their use. They mounted and safely completed the journey.

Hughes was greeted warmly by the Company B commander. "You can speak their language,

John," McDonald said. "I don't know what they've got in their minds."

It was nearing dusk, and groups of men were standing on the streets. The scene reminded Captain Hughes of an earlier day in that same town when he had led Customs Inspector Sabre safely through a hostile mob. With his rifle over his arm, and his pistol in plain view, Hughes walked slowly through the streets. His stern countenance was a warning that if he gave orders, he expected them obeyed.

The Border Boss nodded and spoke to acquaintances as he passed each little group, sometimes in English and sometimes in Spanish. "*Buenas noches,* Pedro . . . hello, Mike . . ." He paused to chat with the men he knew as leaders. He gave each the same message. "I don't want any trouble—tell the men to go home."

The streets were practically deserted within a short time. It was apparent that there would be no more trouble in Rio Grande City—certainly not as long as the Boss was there.

This account of the battle in which the four men were killed disagrees in some details with other published accounts. It is based on the information related to General Hulen and Captain Hughes upon their arrival at the scene. Some months later a Mexican gunman was arrested, and accused of being the assassin of Judge Welch. He was defended by a prominent valley attorney, and was acquitted. No other arrests were made, and the case remained unsolved.

Captain Hughes was on duty at Ranger Headquarters in Austin at the time of this rioting. From 1905 to 1907 he served as a trouble shooter, being sent from Austin to any section of the state where his services were needed. He was on the border again in 1908, and a year later was sent to Amarillo, with orders from the Governor to put an end to the bootlegging of whisky there.

Hughes had been Superintendent of a Sunday School near his Ysleta camp—but chasing bootleggers was a job that did not appeal to him. The work had to be done, though, and he and his men pitched in. They built up the cases and then turned them over to local officers. In a space of a few months they thus caused the arrest of 170 prohibition law violators.

While stationed in Amarillo, the captain sent two of his men, Privates C. R. Moore and Harry Moore to the town of Coahoma, to settle a feud which was boiling there. (The two officers were not related, although their surnames were the same. Their Ranger friends called them, respectively, "Little" Moore and "Big" Moore, to avoid confusion.) They settled the trouble, and a short time after their return to Amarillo, Hughes received a resolution drawn up by the Big Spring grand jury, commending the men for their fine work. There was no personal credit for him in the communication, but he was so pleased that he made certain a copy reached the Governor's desk, and that it was entered in the Adjutant General's records.

He had done the same in a similar incident in 1906. While stationed at Austin he had sent Privates Hurf Carnes, J. C. White, and Milam Wright, to keep the peace at the Humble oil fields. They held off more than three hundred enraged strikers before the controversy was settled, and the oil company wrote Hughes, praising the bravery of the privates in glowing terms.

His subordinates had many similar evidences of the captain's loyalty and affection for them. Pat Craighead, a Ranger not even in his company at the time, was another he befriended. Craighead, with Ranger A. B. Carnes, Deputy Sheriff M. Lawrence, and Earl West, a cowboy, were ambushed while scouting for a gang of Mexican payroll bandits near San Benito one evening. Carnes and Lawrence were killed. West was wounded in the arm, but volunteered to ride to town to summon county officers while Craighead remained on guard at the scene.

The Ranger crouched in the bushes beside the trail, ready to continue the fight if the Mexicans returned, and did not emerge until he heard the possemen coming from town. As he stepped into the trail, the excited officers opened fire and he suffered a wound in the left leg which necessitated amputation just below the knee.

Craighead was recuperating in a hospital when the Ranger force was reduced to two companies. His company was abolished and his name dropped from the roster with the others. Hughes heard about it, protested to the Governor, and Craighead was kept on the payroll and transferred to Hughes' command.

The captain's affection for his men continued even after he had retired from the force, and in 1916 he seriously considered picking up his weapons again and starting out alone to round-up the desperate gang of outlaws which had ambushed and murdered Joe Sitters, a gallant border officer whom Hughes had enlisted in Company D.

Joe Sitters was a great border fighter, and men familiar with his capabilities were unanimous in calling him one of the finest officers ever commissioned along the Rio Grande. He was an expert frontiersman, and his friends boasted that he was talented enough to "track a jack-rabbit through a rock quarry."

Sitters' career began when he was appointed a deputy sheriff in his home county. A short time later, Hughes enlisted him as a private, and he won acclaim in a fight with outlaws less than twenty-four hours after his name was entered on the Ranger roster. Within a few weeks Hughes considered him one of the most efficient officers in Company D.

About this time a desk-trained official in Washington decreed that the U. S. Customs Inspectors along the Mexican border must pass rigid civil service examinations to hold their positions. The Rio Grande river guards were experts when it came to fighting smugglers, but many were short on book learning and were ousted from the service when they failed in written tests. Eastern dudes were sent to replace them.

Soon every day was a field day for the smugglers. They hauled loads of contraband across the river almost at will, and when the Rangers did not stop them, usually returned with a herd of stolen animals. Stockmen sent bitter complaints to Washington, and finally a customs official called upon Captain Hughes and begged for the names of a few good border fighters who might put an end to the wide-spread outlawry.

The salary of customs inspectors was more than twice that of Ranger privates, and when Sitters and another Company D Ranger expressed a desire to transfer, the captain did nothing to stop them. The customs official had not been on the border long enough to know of Sitters' reputation, but enlisted him upon Hughes' recommendation, and immediately gave him the job of rounding up a gang of smugglers who had routed a party of dude-inspectors about three weeks earlier. None of the dudes had been able to follow the trail of the "wet steers" the smugglers had brought into Texas.

It was in February, the month of high winds along the border, and the trail was three weeks old when Sitters picked it up at the river. The other customs men could see no traces of the hoof-prints. The expert located a mark here, and a broken twig there, and followed such scattered tracks for miles through the mountains and across the range. Finally he led his companions to a pasture where the stolen animals were grazing.

The smugglers' holiday was soon over, after the ex-Rangers and a few other good border men got on the job. The Chico Cano gang of smugglers, whose stronghold lay in the mountains across the river from El Porvenir, remained active, however, and Inspector Sitters engaged them in many fights. At length the fierce bandit leader sent word that he, personally, would kill the river guard when next they met.

Sitters, Customs Inspector Joe Howard, and J. A. Harvick, a cattle inspector, were scouting on January 23, 1913, when they flushed a half dozen horsemen in the mountains near the river. They gave chase and captured one of the six when his pony fell. He proved to be Chico Cano.

Sitters disarmed the enraged outlaw, and taunted him about his threats. The officers realized they would have trouble in getting the prisoner safely out of the mountains and prepared for a fight—which was not long in coming. Cano's men opened fire from safe hiding places behind rocks. When the smoke cleared, Inspector Howard was dead, Harvick was shot through the leg, and Sitters was unconscious with a wound in the head. Cano escaped.

The bullet had only creased Joe's skull, and he was soon back in saddle. When Cano learned this he again sent threats across the river, but did not appear to back them up in person. Sitters bore a charmed life for more than three years—until May 24, 1916. On that date he was again ambushed. He and Ranger Eugene Hulen, brother of the Adjutant General, were riding through a narrow canyon some distance away from their companions. Hulen was killed instantly, and when Sitters' body was found it was riddled with bullets, the flesh torn to shreds, and his face beaten to a pulp by rocks, boot heels and gun-butts.

Perhaps that was Chico Cano's revenge.

CHAPTER XII

PRESIDENT PORFIRIO DIAZ ruled the excitable Mexican *peons* with an iron hand for nearly thirty-five years, but the bitter Orozco-Madero revolution in 1910 finally led to his resignation, and chaos, a year later. During the next four years, the Republic of Mexico had nine presidents, one of whom held office less than half an hour.

Captain Hughes' intimate knowledge of people and affairs south of the border was invaluable to Texas officials during these troubled years, and frequently his views were relayed to the State Department at Washington, where they were considered in the formulating of mayor policies.

The Texas authorities had expected border incidents during the Spanish-American War, and had increased the Ranger force at that time. But Diaz was in power then and the extra officers were not needed. Now, with the federal government demoralized below the Rio Grande, it appeared certain that there would be trouble along the border—and unfortunately, the Ranger force had just been reduced to only two companies of about a half dozen men each. Moreover, the state budget did not allow for the hiring of additional officers.

Governor Colquitt, genuinely alarmed, made urgent representations to Washington, and President Taft was so impressed by the dangers confronting the citizens of Texas that he requested the Congress to appropriate $10,000 to apply on salaries and expenses of Rangers assigned to duty on the north bank of the river boundary. A check for a sum just short of that amount was dully received in Austin, and credited to the Ranger account. Captain Hughes, recently appointed Senior Captain of the force, was sent to the border and instructed to enlist such additional men as he needed.

When Hughes reached his Ysleta camp, he

learned that a revolutionary army was marching in the direction of Juarez, and quickly reported to the Governor that a clash was imminent, and that it was more than likely that cannon shells might fall in El Paso, endangering the lives and property of Texas citizens. Governor Colquitt kept in personal touch with Hughes during this period, and some of the chief executive's communications are of historical interest.

Following is his reply to this report from the Ranger commander:

EXECUTIVE OFFICE
STATE OF TEXAS
AUSTIN, TEXAS

May 15, 1911

Hon. John R. Hughes,
Capt., Company A,
Ysleta, Texas.

Dear Sir:

I have your letter of May 12th.

In view of conditions prevailing at Juarez I wish you would take as many of your men as convenient and remain in El Paso until matters quiet down. I want you especially to remain in El Paso as my special representative and keep me advised by wire of the situation if there is danger of a conflict.

I will look into the law and see what right the Governor of this State has to require of the combatants that they do not shoot into the city of El Paso. Please proceed to El Paso upon receipt of this letter and remain there until further advised.

Yours truly,

(Signed)   O. B. Colquitt
GOVERNOR

It will be noticed that Captain Hughes was addressed as Captain of Company A. Companies C and D had been dropped when the Ranger force was reduced shortly prior to this date, but the roster of Company A was made up of the same men who had served under Hughes for several years.

The Ranger camp was moved from Ysleta to El Paso upon the same date that this letter was received. Subsequently, Hughes was ordered back to Austin, where his advice was more easily available to the Governor and other officials. However, he remained in close contact with his men on the border, and made frequent trips there. Juarez was the scene of fighting after the Rangers reached El Paso, but so far as is known, no shells fell north of the Rio Grande at this time.

As the Governor's personal representative, Hughes was required to keep in close touch with developments across the river, and he frequently consulted with some of the revolutionary leaders, to ascertain their plans for the future. About a year later, charges were made that the Texas Rangers were endangering United States neutrality in the Mexican conflicts by "associating" with the revolutionists, notably General Francisco Villa.

The reports reached Washington, and the same Congress which had solicited the Rangers' aid seriously debated the question of whether or not the Ranger force might actually "declare war upon Mexico," notwithstanding the fact that the force consisted of only about twenty officers at that time.

Governor Colquitt's letters about this were of special interest. The first follows:

GOVERNOR'S OFFICE
AUSTIN, TEXAS

March 23, 1912

Capt. John R. Hughes,
El Paso, Texas.
Dear Sir:

Your letter of March 20, with clipping from the El Paso Times, is received.

Please keep me advised of all information obtainable by you, but I wish to call your attention to the fact that the United States Government has not recognized the belligerency of the revolutionary forces in Mexico, and I suggest, therefore, that you do not have any conferences with revolutionary leaders, as it would subject us to criticism of encouraging enemies of the Government of Mexico.

Yours truly,
(Signed) O. B. Colquitt
GOVERNOR

On the afternoon of that same day, the Governor addressed another, and stronger, communication to the Senior Captain, as follows:

GOVERNOR'S OFFICE
AUSTIN, TEXAS

March 23, 1912

Capt. John R. Hughes,
El Paso, Texas.
Dear Sir:

Further referring to your letter of March 20, to which I made answer this morning, I had a conference at noon with the Mexican Consul at San Antonio.

I learn through him that it is being charged that the Rangers are in sympathy with the Revolutionists in

Mexico. I explained to him that I knew that this was not true, and that I had given orders through the Adjutant General that the Rangers take no part in, or express any partisan preference in the politics or affairs of Mexico.

I sincerely trust that you will see that your men observe this injunction. In my letter to you this morning I called attention to the fact that the United States Government had not recognized the revolutionists in Mexico as belligerents. This is to advise you, therefore, that they are not entitled to be so considered by you, or any other officer of this state, and I enjoin upon you that you hold no conference or correspondence with any revolutionary leader.

I am sending a copy of this letter to Adjutant General Hutchings with request that he communicate a copy of it to each of the Ranger captains.

Yours truly,

(Signed) O. B. Colquitt
GOVERNOR

Captain Hughes had at no time expressed partisanship in affairs across the river, and his only purpose in conferring with Villa, and other leaders, was to obtain advance information concerning impending battles, and to repeat over and over again strongly worded warnings against the revolutionists allowing their gunfire to carry across the border. The Captain so reported to Governor Colquitt, and the incident was closed a few days later, as follows:

GOVERNOR'S OFFICE
AUSTIN, TEXAS

March 28, 1912

Capt. John R. Hughes,
El Paso, Texas.
Dear Captain:

I acknowledge your letter of March 20, and I am glad

to receive it. I have called upon the Mexican Consul, at the request of the Adjutant General, to be informed of the source of his information as to the attitude of the Texas Rangers toward the Mexican Revolution.

I notice that he is leaving for Mexico City. He told me in person that some man, who had come from Washington City, reported to him that such information had reached the National Capital.

I will send a copy of your letter to his office, and ask him to forward a copy to President Madero.

Yours truly,

(Signed) O. B. Colquitt
GOVERNOR

There was another lull in activities along the border, and then Captain Hughes, in camp again at Ysleta, received information that revolutionists were camping on "Pirate Island," and threatening to cross into the United States to make raids and replenish their food supplies. Just at that time, too, the federal government had made arrangements to pass a division of Mexican troops through Texas, and the Captain felt it expedient that a representative of the Governor be present, even though United States soldiers were handling the matter.

Captain Hughes left for El Paso with two men, and sent Ranger Sergeant C. R. Moore and Private Pat Craighead, who were in San Elizario, to verify the presence of the revolutionists on the island. The sergeant and Craighead found traces of an abandoned camp, and took custody of one man they suspected of being a revolutionist. Captain Hughes included a report of their findings, along with his own from El Paso:

El Paso, Texas,
Sept. 12, 1912

The Governor,
Austin, Texas.

Sir:

I came to El Paso last night to watch the passage of Mexican troops through the state of Texas. One troop train passed yesterday evening about 4:45, another about 2:40 this morning. A Ranger accompanied each train through the state. The guns of these soldiers were carried in a baggage car, and were in charge of United States troops. This is all the Mexican troops that will move through the state at this time.

Two members of my company, Sergeant Moore and Private Craighead, started from San Elizario to Pirate Island, thirty miles below El Paso, yesterday, and captured one revolutionist, who is now in jail in El Paso. It was reported that there had been forty revolutionists on this island yesterday, and that they took some horses back to Mexico with them. My men got there a little too late to apprehend the main party, but succeeded in catching the one. They will remain about two days longer on the island.

There is a band of revolutionists on the Mexican side of the Rio Grande, about sixty-five miles below El Paso, and I expect to send a man down there to watch their maneuvers.

I know of no other revolutionists down the river, except the band I last mentioned, and the ones at Ojinaga.

Very respectfully,
(Signed)   John R. Hughes
Captain Company A, Ranger Force.

Sergeant Moore and Private Craighead were, indeed, disappointed that they had not been able to "apprehend the main party" of forty revolutionists. Neither their Captain nor the Governor appeared to doubt that they would have been able to capture all forty, had they found them. The two Rangers remained on the island, scene of the death of Captain Jones, for a couple of days and then returned to camp. They were in constant danger of attack, but were confident they could out-fight any number of men who might come at them. Perhaps their possible opponents agreed, for there was no trouble.

Captain Hughes had no more than mailed this report when he received information that the revolutionist Orozco and a few confederates had been captured by United States officers when they had crossed the Rio Grande in the Big Bend area. He hastened there and when the Mexicans were released, made a report to the Governor. He was incensed that the federal government could be so lenient with the men when their mere presence north of the river was a threat to the security of Texas citizens.

Governor Colquitt shared his views, and indicated that the state of Texas would take independent action from the United States Government, if need be, when he acknowledged the report:

GOVERNOR'S OFFICE
AUSTIN, TEXAS

Sept. 23, 1912

Capt. John R. Hughes,
Marfa, Texas.

Dear Captain:

I have your letter of September 19th, also yours of the 15th, concerning your activities in the Marfa and Presidio section.

I note that the United States Commissioner at Marfa discharged Orozco and associates, finding them not guilty of violating the neutrality laws, but they were rearrested upon complaint of the Mexican Consul. If the United States Government releases these men, and if the Mexican Consul will make complaint against them, arrest and hold them for further directions.

I am thinking of increasing your company so that you may keep a detail at Marfa or Presidio to watch the situation. I would like to have your opinion of this matter without delay.

Yours truly,

(Signed)   O. B. Colquitt

GOVERNOR

The Mexican Consul was not available to make a state complaint against the revolutionists, and they finally got back across the river, but not before Captain Hughes had given them solemn warning that he would take prompt action if they, or any of their men, interfered with the rights of Texas citizens.

Hughes could always be found at the danger spots along the border in the El Paso region, and he was always prepared to fight to protect the lives and property of the people of his state, regardless of what action was taken by the federal authorities charged with protecting the interests of all United States citizens. Soon he was given proper recognition as an authority on Mexican affairs and at length the United States Department of State took note of his advice. Governor Colquitt indicated his pleasure in the following letter to the captain:

GOVERNOR'S OFFICE
AUSTIN, TEXAS

October 28, 1912

Capt. John R. Hughes,
El Paso, Texas.

Dear Sir:

Referring to your letter of October 21 which reached me on the day I was leaving for Dallas, I quoted your former letter about the situation around El Paso in a letter I wrote to the President, in which I requested him to adopt measures to give full protection to the Texas people.

I notice by the morning papers that General Steever has tightened up the situation. I presume he has received fresh instructions from Washington as a result of my letter to the President.

Keep me posted as to the situation.

Yours truly,

(Signed) O. B. Colquitt
GOVERNOR

Since the United States Government had not recognized the belligerency of the Orozco army, federal troops gave no formal attention to the maneuvers of the revolutionist. But the Texas Rangers did. Orozco's troops were marching along the south bank of the Rio Grande, and Captain Hughes detailed men to march opposite them along the north bank, to make certain that the Mexican soldiers did not cross, or even fire across, the border.

Orozco had a large force of men. True to the Ranger code, Captain Hughes relied upon two of his men to handle them all. Sergeant Moore and Private Charles Webster marched opposite the Orozco army, with as much formality as though they were accompanied by a regiment of cavalry.

Governor Colquitt also relied upon the two Rangers, and in a letter to Hughes instructed them to deal firmly with the revolutionist if he dared venture into Texas. The letter takes formal notice of the work of Moore and Webster, and the entire incident thus becomes another inspiring chapter in Ranger tradition. It follows:

GOVERNOR'S OFFICE
AUSTIN, TEXAS

August 26, 1912

Capt. John R. Hughes,
Ysleta, Texas.

Dear Sir:

I have your letter of August 22nd, advising me of the report made to you by Sergeant Moore and Private Webster, who have been marching parallel to a rebel force under Orozco along the Rio Grande river.

I trust you will keep me posted as to the movements of the revolutionists and keep a strict look out, and if Orozco crosses into Texas take him into custody at once and report to me.

Feeling assured of your vigilance, I am

Yours truly,
(Signed)   O. B. Colquitt
GOVERNOR

The two Rangers did not clash with the Mexican army on this occasion. Orozco completed his march, and the officers returned to the Ysleta camp. Later, however, Captain Hughes heard that a rebel band under General José Ynez Salazar was threatening a raid across the border, and he again dispatched Moore and

Webster to engage them, if and when the revolutionists set foot on Texas soil.

The Rangers located the rebels opposite the
Big Bend, and took position on the north bank.
A half dozen soldiers started across the river
two days later, and the Rangers ordered them
to turn back. Taken by surprise, the soldiers
turned their ponies and fled.

The two Rangers, accompanied by a deputy
sheriff, followed the little army up the river a
short distance. Suddenly the whole company
started to ford the stream. The Texas officers
dodged behind a pile of rocks which would
give them protection, and Sergeant Moore chal-
lenged the group.

"Halt!" he commanded.

The rebels pulled in their ponies, and suddenly opened fire. The sergeant and his companions looked to their own weapons and their
first three shots toppled three Mexicans from
their saddles.

Ignoring the commands of their officers the
soldiers broke ranks and raced their horses back
to the shelter of the trees on the south bank.
The Texans expected another attack, but it did
not come, and later they discovered that the
Mexicans had retired to the deep interior.

Captain Hughes reported the incident to
Austin by telegraph, and forwarded details by
letter. Governor Colquitt, in his reply firmly
reiterated that the state of Texas, through the
Rangers, would remain prepared at any time to
act independently in protecting its integrity,

and guarding the safety of its citizens. His historically important letter follows:

GOVERNOR'S OFFICE
AUSTIN, TEXAS

February 3, 1913

Capt. John R. Hughes,
El Paso, Texas.

Dear Captain:

Your letter of January 30 to the Adjutant General has been referred by him to me.

You give an account of the experience of Sergeant Moore and Private Webster and Deputy Sheriff Garlick in their brush with the rebels. I think the time has come when the State should not hesitate to deal with these marauding bands of rebels in a way which they will understand. I approve the course of Sergeant Moore and Private Webster in this incident, and I instruct you and your men to keep them off of Texas territory if possible, and if they invade the State let them understand they do so at the risk of their lives.

Yours truly,
(Signed)   O. B. Colquitt
GOVERNOR

Armed with this authority, Captain Hughes kept his men ready to fight at any time, but there were only a few isolated incidents in his territory after that. It was anticipated that there might be trouble when the United States seized Vera Cruz in 1914, but none developed. Men under Captain Hughes' command never again were required to engage the rebels.

While protecting the neutrality of Texas, Hughes discovered that many of the Mexican outlaws who had operated along the border were playing prominent roles in the revolutions, among them his old enemy, Antonio Carrasco.

The fierce bandit leader had long since ceased sending assassins after Hughes' scalp, principally because he could not find men foolhardy enough to accept such a hopeless assignment.

Carrasco led his followers into the Orozco-Madero war. He claimed the title of General and might have climbed to high position, but he made the error of attempting to serve both sides. In the spring of 1911, and at the order of Francisco I. Madero, he and his lieutenants died before a firing squad, at the insurrecto army camp of General José de la Cruz Sanchez.

These and similar executions benefited Texas law enforcement officers, but the revolutions made the Rangers' work more difficult by destroying the national police force which fought the outlaws south of the border. President Diaz, during the late years of his reign, established an organization similar to the Texas Rangers, which was called the Guardia Rural, or more commonly, the *rurales*. The chief was Col. Emilio Kosterlitzky, who had once been a corporal in the United States army, and it was said that he had command of 1,200 officers.

Kosterlitzky was an honest official, and utterly ruthless when it came to dealing with outlaws. There were few reliable courts of justice in northern Mexico, so he made arrests, tried the prisoners himself, and either executed or released them.

The Guardia Rural was dissolved when Diaz left office, and Kosterlitzky fled to the United

States. He was Agent in Charge of the U. S. Secret Service office at Los Angeles when he died in 1928. Captain Hughes and the Colonel never met, but while engaged on opposite sides of the border they frequently exchanged information and greetings through emissaries.

Hughes became well acquainted with another Mexican celebrity, however. He and Pancho Villa met many times before the Rangers received orders from Austin not to recognize the rebels. Hughes discovered that many of the widely circulated stories about Villa were false, notably the gossip about the bandit's drunkenness. Pancho, himself, was not a drinking man, although those around him were often intoxicated. Sometimes brutal and incapable, he was nevertheless a conscientious leader of his people, in Hughes' opinion. He once told the captain:

"I'd be a hell of a fellow to be president—not able to read or write."

The desperado was born in the mountains of Durango state, the son of an impoverished Indian *peon*, Hughes learned. His true name was Doroteo Aranga. It was not until he became a bandit leader that he began calling himself Francisco "Pancho" Villa.

When he was fourteen, young Aranga ran away from home after a series of unpleasant experiences with the wealthy land owner who held his parents in virtual slavery. He would have perished in the mountains had he not been found and adopted by a bandit chieftain. He demonstrated his fearlessness in raids upon caravans and *haciendas,* and when the leader was mortally wounded in a gun-fight, he named Pancho his successor. So, at 17, Villa was supreme ruler of a dangerous gang of thieves.

About a year later he visited his parents and learned that his fifteen-year-old sister had been ravished by an army captain, the son of the land owner who then employed the girl's father. Pancho lay in wait for the young officer, lassoed him with a rawhide *riata,* and galloped away dragging his victim over the rocky mountain slope.

The body was mutilated almost beyond recognition when it was finally found, and the young man's father offered a reward of 10,000 *pesos* for Villa. But Pancho remained at large, and continued to rob and plunder, endearing himself to the *peons* by stealing only from the rich.

A deserter from his gang once joined the *rurales* and boasted that he would "cut out Pancho's heart" when they met. By this time there was an enormous price on Villa's head, but he appeared in the city of Chihuahua and surprised the braggard lounging in front of a shop. Pancho put four bullets into his abdomen —placing them there so that he would "die in agony"—and galloped safely away.

Carranza and Villa fought side by side as revolutionists, but spilt when the United States aided the former. Pancho was enraged by this

Washington policy, and was thus inspired to lead his infamous raid upon Columbus, New Mexico, and to terrorize other border communities. Hughes believed that the assassins who finally killed Villa, after he had eluded General Pershing's expeditionary force, were hired by high Mexican government officials.

The captain's views about the bandit leader were often sought in later years, and he never hesitated to express his firm conviction that Pancho, despite his bad deeds, had at least two redeeming characteristics: he never went back on his word, and never proved traitor to a friend. It was his loyalty, perhaps, that especially appealed to Hughes. The captain held that trait as the first requisite of any man he called friend.

CHAPTER XIII

CAPTAIN HUGHES WAS A competent, thorough peace officer at all times and in every locality, but his first love was the border country and it was there that his services were of inestimable value. Even as Senior Captain, assigned to duty in Austin, he kept detachments under his personal command at Ysleta and Marfa, and was never really happy unless he was present to lead these men on their lonely, dangerous scouts along the Rio Grande.

He was, primarily, a frontiersman, particularly adept at tracking and in the lore of living and fighting in the uncharted wilds. As the border country became more settled, these talents were not as greatly needed in the Ranger service. Automobiles supplanted horses, and outlaws no longer maintained permanent strongholds in the mountains or river valleys, nor could they be trailed by hoof-marks across the open range.

In bowing to progress, the captain had the feeling that his type of "horseback Ranger" duty was no longer needed, and finally he announced that he would retire at the change of state administrations in 1915. His men begged him to reconsider, and to please them he made a tentative overture to James E. Ferguson, the Governor-elect, and learned that the new executive intended a clean sweep of state offices, to make room for appointees of his own choosing.

So on January 31, 1915, Captain John R. Hughes, the Border Boss, resigned from the Ranger force which he had served so faithfully for twenty-eight years—nearly twenty-two years of that time as Captain. He was then.sixty years old, and he had been longer a Ranger and longer a captain than any other man.

State newspapers decried the loss to Texas, but the editors and the public agreed that he had well earned the right to lay aside his arduous tasks. In recalling his record for their readers, some of the editors dug into the reports in the Adjutant General's office, and found revealing statistics.

The Adjutant General's statement of the accomplishments of the Ranger force for one two-year period showed, for example, that Captain Hughes and his Company D men had led the entire organization in number of arrests for murder, for aggravated assault, stock thievery, swindling, robbery, rape, smuggling, minor offenses, and in total arrests. They had recovered twice as much stolen stock as any other company, and rode their horses a total of 388,463 miles on scouts and other official business.

The figures were not the same for every two-year period, but his Company D men were never far from the top.

As a Ranger commander, Hughes' salary had been $100 a month, plus expenses. Always thrifty, he had begun buying property in the vicinity of Ysleta, and near the Rio Grande, when he was first detailed to duty there in 1895. Before his retirement he had acquired extensive holdings, much of which he had purchased at three dollars and four dollars an acre. He had built a couple of adobe buildings to serve as Company D headquarters, and planned to make his home in one of them when he was free to live the life of a simple rancher.

Construction of the great Elephant Butte dam in southern New Mexico changed all of this. His land was adjacent to well-flooded irrigation ditches, and he sold it for farming purposes, receiving $100 and more per acre.

So when he retired from the Ranger force, Captain Hughes had a yearly income far in excess of his salary as senior commander. He put out the money at good interest, and doubled and tripled the principal. The financial upheaval of 1929 cut into his investments, and "did him no good," he admitted, but he was left with a life income well beyond his needs.

When newspapers throughout the country announced his retirement, motion picture company officials, writers, and promoters, flocked around him. To escape them he began a leisurely tour of the United States, visited Cuba and Canada, and finally reached the ranch home of his old Ranger friend, Ira Aten, in California. He returned there a half-dozen winters, and frequently the two old friends met for vacations together in the summer months.

The captain never married. He told many interviewers that a man living the dangerous, uncertain life of a Ranger along the border had no right to marry, but Aten was authority for the statement that the tragic death of Elizabeth Todd was largely responsible for his remaining a bachelor. In later years the captain, always with a chuckle, blamed women for most of the troubles of the world—but he had a sharp eye for the charms of pretty girls, and thoroughly enjoyed their company.

At his retirement, the veteran Ranger had lost little of his vigor and zest for excitement and action. Naturally, his days of idleness, with only his investments to look after, sometimes grew irksome. He tried prospecting for awhile, in the Hueco Mountains, northeast of El Paso. He panned a small amount of dust, turned-up a few gold nuggets under his pick-axe, but benefited mostly from the exercise and mental relaxation. He once stumbled onto an abandoned shaft in what appeared to have been a rich vein, and his Indian guide grudgingly asserted it was the famous old Padre mine, lost for generations. Not especially interested at the time, the white man did not mark the location, and could never find it again.

Hughes lost touch with his family while still a boy in Indian Territory, and as an adult felt no close ties of kinship. He outlived all of his brothers who, like himself, became leaders in their respective communities. William P. Hughes was editor and publisher of a newspaper, and United States Commissioner, at Newport, Washington, near the Canadian border. The captain was with him in Austin in 1878, and did not see him again until 1937.

As a Ranger commander, Hughes frequently wore a mustache, and after his retirement he raised a full beard. Tall, erect, neatly dressed, distinguished looking, he was always a commanding figure. Sometimes his sombrero was adorned with a string of beads instead of a cloth or cord band—beads that were a treasured gift when he was a boy with the Indians.

In later years he wore a patch over his left ear. A tick crawled into it one night in '89, while he was sleeping on the range. The insect died there, and the only available physician could not remove it. Fifty years later, the ear was almost constantly inflamed, and the captain's hearing was slightly impaired.

This and his bent right arm were his only scars. He could use the arm to a limited extent, but there was little strength in it and the fingers did not respond well to impulses.

Only an unusually hardy man could have stood up, as Hughes did, for so many years under the hardships and nervous strain of an old-time Ranger's life, and retire with unimpaired health. When scouting alone, he frequently was away from camp for weeks at a time, without sleeping more than a few minutes in any twenty-four hour period. Guards were posted at night when there were several officers in the posse, but the captain was so attuned to being wide awake at the first movement around him that he slept little even under such conditions.

"I made up for it, though," he explained. "In camp I could roll up in my blanket and be dead for twelve or fifteen hours at a time."

After his retirement, El Paso was home to the captain, as much as any one community was, but in later years he divided his time, when he was not traveling outside the state, between that city and Austin, where he helped organize and was for several years chairman of the board of directors, and largest single stockholder, of the Citizens Industrial Bank.

He was a frequent and welcome visitor to

state offices in Austin, and in El Paso no civic celebration was complete unless he rode at the head of the parade or sat among the honored guests. He was unofficial greeter for the El Paso Chamber of Commerce, being drafted by the secretary to help entertain celebrities who visited the Gateway City.

CHAPTER XIV

I MET CAPTAIN HUGHES for the first time in Austin, and was with him later in El Paso, a few weeks before he celebrated his eighty-fifth birthday anniversary, on February 11, 1940. He was, I discovered, as active and spry as many a man of fifty. He had the peculiar, teetering walk of one who had spent many years in a saddle, but his life on the open range seemed only to have toughened his rugged physique. His eyes were steady and clear—as sharp as his mind.

He had been twenty-five years a retired Ranger when I first knew him, but the many events of his busy career were sharply etched in his memory. He could tell me the initials and nick-names of obscure officers in his company, and set me right on dates and facts which were not to be found in any reports or histories. His modesty, however, made my work more difficult.

The Ranger commanders of his day where required to make monthly reports of the activities of their men, and these statements, in their own handwriting, are valuable exhibits in the Texas archives at the state library. Stirring fights along the border, in which perhaps a score of shots were exchanged, were given only routine listing, with no mention of the shooting or the dangers involved.

In going through Captain Hughes' reports, I found a brief statement in the one for February, 1903, to the effect that he and some of his men had attended a murder trial in Fredericksburg. There were similar notations in other months, mentioning that Company D men had attended trials, or had guarded railroad trains at the request of Wells Fargo express officials. This one I investigated further, and located a letter from Hughes to the Adjutant General. It read, in part:

". . . went to Fredericksburg to assist the sheriff in keeping the peace at district court during the trial of Sam Lochlin, who was being tried for murder. The case being a change

of venue from Llano County, a number of
witnesses from surrounding counties were in attendance, some of whom were said to be dangerous characters.

"We stayed in Fredericksburg until court
was over and Lochlin was convicted of murder
in the first degree and sentenced to the peniten-
tiary for life. *We succeeded in keeping the peace.*
From there, assisted by Private A. R. Mace, I
helped the deputy sheriff take the prisoner,
Lochlin, to San Antonio, where he was placed
in jail for safe keeping. We then returned to
headquarters at Alice."

One sentence in this report stood out, although the italics are mine. "We succeeded in
keeping the peace." I questioned the captain as
to what that success had entailed, and he brush-
ed aside the entire incident as "unimportant."
I obtained the full details from other sources,
and then realized that many of Hughes' most
daring adventures actually seemed unimportant
to him.

It was openly announced before this murder
trial began that one faction or the other, de-
pending upon how the jury voted, would open
a gun-fight. Feeling was intense between the
two camps. Rangers shadowed the principals
on both sides, and managed to keep tempers
unruffled.

Several groups of peace officers were present
as witnesses, and one night a sheriff from a distant county staggered out of a saloon to weave
through the streets in search of a rival officer

who was a witness for the opposing faction. A gun-fight was in prospect and frightened townspeople ran to cover.

Captain Hughes was summoned, and he hastened to intercept the enraged man. They met on a sidewalk in the business district, and as the Ranger advanced, the intoxicated officer put his hand in position for a quick draw.

"Take it easy—we don't want any trouble here," Hughes said, calmly. Holding the officer's eyes with a stern gaze, he walked up to him, and with a single quick movement took possession of his six-shooter.

Everyone knows that a Texas officer will fight to the bitter end before he will surrender his weapon, but this sheriff not only allowed himself to be disarmed, but made no loud objection when the Ranger commander kept the pistol for the duration of the trial. Intoxicated or sober, he had no desire to tangle with the Border Boss.

The Rangers expected a show-down when the jury returned the verdict, but they stood in the aisles between the rival groups, and quickly hustled the Lochlin supporters out of the courtroom. No weapons appeared. It was largely Hughes' reputation as a fighter, and the certain knowledge that he had never given up a prisoner, which kept an angry mob of citizens from attempting to seize and lynch the condemned man.

Incidents like this seemed unimportant to old Rangers, but to most present-day civilians the dangers the officers encountered in a single episode would be adventure enough for a lifetime.

I was curious as to what precautions were taken by the old-time Rangers when, traveling alone, they were faced with the task of transporting one or more prisoners through the unsettled frontier. When Captain Hughes had an outlaw in custody and no one to assist him, he often went days at a time without resting. But sometimes he hid his weapons, handcuffed the prisoner's arm to his own, and made the outlaw stretch out on the ground beside him while he snatched a few minutes sleep. He might have handcuffed him to a tree or bush, but preferred keeping him close at hand.

"Of course, I made certain there wasn't a rock or anything else handy that would give him an advantage," he explained.

It was typical of Hughes that he never doubted his ability to arouse himself in time to emerge the victor in a hand-to-hand struggle, should the captive attempt to overpower him. He did not mention it, but the most dangerous outlaws usually were meek and tractable while in his custody.

Ranger Ira Aten had an amusing experience while scouting alone, and Hughes enjoyed telling me about it. Riding down a lonely trail one evening, in the heart of the outlaw country along the Rio Grande, Aten came upon another lone traveler, frying side meat over a fire. The stranger, an elderly man, invited him to dismount and share the meal, and he accepted. The civilian did not identify himself, and neither did the Ranger.

After the meal, they sat before the fire chatting. It was wisdom not to ask questions of strangers in that territory, and both were cautious in that respect. They were ready to roll up in their blankets, but neither was certain it would be safe—that the other did not have murder and robbery in mind.

Aten finally made the first move. He stretched out beside the smouldering fire, but took the precaution of removing his pistol from its holster, and holding it in his hand beneath the blanket. As he watched the stranger, who was straightening out his own blankets, he dosed for a few moments, and awoke with a start at the sound of a voice. The old man was kneeling a short distance away, praying earnestly to be delivered from any outlaw who was close at hand.

"That was enough for Aten—he never had a better night's sleep on the trail," Hughes chuckled.

The captain celebrated his eighty-sixth birthday anniversary in Austin, with the aged widow of his printer-brother, and her children—his nieces and nephews. I was with him often during this period, and gained a glimpse of a sentimental side of his character, revealed to few. He showed me a notebook which he had carried for many years as a Ranger. Some of the pages he had used for keeping his accounts. But

on most were copied down verses, particularly
the words of old cowboy songs, which had appealed to him.

One of his favorites was called "The Texas
Ranger." It was composed by the step-mother
of one of his Ranger privates, and transcribed
in the notebook in her handwriting. "The
Texas Ranger" also was reproduced in the
diary and scrapbook of Lon Oden, Hughes' old
Ranger companion, which was edited and published a number of years ago by Oden's
daughter. It follows:

He leaves unplowed his furrow,
    He leaves his book unread,
For a life of tented freedom
    By lure of danger led.
He's first in the hour of peril,
    He's gayest in the dance,
Like the guardsman of old England,
    Or the beau sabreur of France.

He stands our faithful bulwark
    Against the savage foe;
Through lonely woodland places
    Our children come and go.
Our flocks and herds untended
    O'er hill and valley roam;
The Ranger in the saddle
    Means peace for us at home.

Behold our smiling farmsteads,
    Where waves the golden grain!
Beneath yon tree earth's bosom
    Was dark with crimson stain;
That bluff the death shot echoed
    Of husband, father, slain—
God grant such sights of horror
    We never see again.

The gay and hardy Ranger
  His blanket on the ground,
Lies by the blazing campfire,
  While song and tale go round;
And if one voice is silent—
  One fails to hear the jest—
They know his thoughts are absent
  With her who loves him best.

Our State, her sons confess it,
  That queenly, star-crowned brow,
Has darkened 'neath the shadow
  Of lawlessness ere now;
And men of evil passions
  On her reproach had laid,
But that the ready Ranger
  Rode promptly to her aid.

He may not win the laurels,
  Nor trumpet tongue of fame,
But beauty smiles upon him,
  And ranchmen bless his name.
Then here's to the Texas Ranger,
  Past, present and to come,
Our safety from the savage,
  The guardian of our home.

*   *   *   *   *   *

Also in the notebook were often quoted lines
of an old Texan which were fancied by the captain:

When my soul seeks range and rest,
  Beyond the last divide,
Just plant me in some stretch of West
  That's sunny, lone and wide.
Let cattle rub my tombstone down;
  And coyotes mourn their kin.
Let hawses paw and tromp the moun'
  But don't you fence it in!

Many of the verses were set down in the neat penmanship of feminine hands, and this verified the statements of his old associates that the handsome, gallant and famous Ranger hero had many romantic admirers among the gentler sex. Photographs of beautiful young ladies were pasted on a few of the pages, and preserved inside the cover was a small buckskin bag, trimmed with colored beads crudely outlining the initial J. It was made for Hughes by an Indian girl while he was living among the Osages. He carried it with him for nearly seventy years.

Old associates recalled that the captain had a few favorites among the young women of El Paso, whose names were frequently coupled with his. He laughingly verified this, and admitted that there was one in particular to whom he once made the gift of a saddle pony. "That was the only horse I ever stole," he chuckled.

As a Ranger commander, he kept four or five mounts at camp for his own use, but for more than eight years he was usually seen riding a zebra dun gelding which he called Jack. The horse weighed only 860 pounds, and when his master was astride with heavy saddle, ammunition, weapons and equipment, the little animal was carrying approximately 250 pounds. Jack was greatly admired by other Rangers, who insisted that he would advance on tip-toes when the captain wished to move silently.

The little animal grew old in Hughes' service, and finally he was turned over to the young lady, who promised to give him good care and regular exercise. But Jack liked the range, and even the best of care in a city stable did not agree with him. The captain, moving his company by rail to the Big Bend district, "stole" the pony and turned him loose on a ranch near Marfa, where he spent the rest of his days grazing in freedom on the range.

Captain Hughes purchased an automobile shortly after his retirement from the Ranger force, and even at eighty-seven, he thought nothing of climbing behind the wheel and starting off alone on a thousand mile trip.

He rarely revealed to anyone his proposed date of departure, or his exact destination. He had been too long a bachelor to account for his movements or actions. Also, he had found it prudent as a Ranger commander never to give advance notice to his possible enemies among the outlaw elements as to where he might be found at any given time. This and similar precautions became a habit. For the same reason he was never fully at ease sitting near a window in a lighted room at night, unless the shades were drawn.

As a Ranger, he had been subject to transfer to any part of the state on an hour's notice. He did not acquire more possessions than he could conveniently carry in a couple of traveling cases. Even after his retirement he could easily load all his belongings into his car, and make his home wherever he hung his hat.

Many honors were bestowed upon Captain

Hughes, but in leaving him we shall consider only one, in which he was given national recognition. It came in 1940, when he was eighty-five.

Bernarr Macfadden, the publisher, sponsored a movement to call public attention to the bravery of peace officers of the nation, by citing outstanding heroes of the forty-eight states for their valor in the performance of duty. The citations were made by a distinguished Board of Award, consisting of Lewis J. Valentine, Police Commissioner of New York City; Col. Homer Garrison, Jr., Director of the Texas Department of Public Safety; Chief of Police Edward B. Hansen, of Duluth, Minn., President of the FBI National Police Academy Associates; Publisher Macfadden, and two of his noted editors, Fulton Oursler and John Shuttleworth.

The six members of the board, voting unanimously, selected Captain Hughes as the first recipient of the Certificate of Valor. I was privileged to carry the award to him in Austin, where it was presented by Colonel Garrison in the headquarters office of the Ranger force. The aptly worded citation, signed by the members of the award board, read:

"Whereas, on many notable occasions in your long career as a peace officer, when faced with death in the performance of your duty, you unhesitantly acted in these emergencies with courage and daring; and Whereas, by your heroism and fortitude you have brought honor to your profession and to your fellow officers everywhere, Therefore, we the undersigned commend you and publicly acknowledge your outstanding service to the cause of law enforcement and to good citizenship."

Captain John R. Hughes' outstanding service to the cause of law enforcement and to good citizenship is, indeed, a matter of public record. It will live forever in the pages of Texas history.

BIBLIOGRAPHY

BIBLIOGRAPHY

Barry, Buck.
   A Texas Ranger and Frontiersman, Southwest Press,
   Dallas, 1932.
Bush, Dr. I. J.
   Gringo Doctor, The Caxton Printers, Ltd., Cald-
   well, Idaho, 1939.
Coolidge, Dane.
   Fighting Men of the West, E. P. Dutton & Co.,
   New York, 1932.
Cunningham, Eugene.
   Tiggernometry—A Gallery of Gunfighters, Press of
   the Pioneers, Inc., New York, 1934.
Dixon, Billy.
   Life and Adventures of 'Billy' Dixon, Co-operative
   Publishing Co., Guthrie, Oklahoma, 1914.
Gillett, James B.
   Six Years with the Texas Rangers, 1875-1881, Von
   Boeckmann-Jones Co., Austin, 1921.
Jennings, N. A.
   A Texas Ranger, (reprint) Southwest Press, Dallas,
   1930.
King, W. H.
   The Texas Ranger Service, Scarff, Dallas, 1898.
Maltby, W. J.
   *Capt. Jeff or Frontier Life in Texas with the Texas
   Rangers*, Whipkey Printing Co., Colorado, Texas,
   1906.
Payne, Albert Bigelow.
   Capt. Bill McDonald, Texas Ranger, Little & Ives
   Co., New York, 1909.
Roberts, Mrs. D. W.
   *A Woman's Reminiscences of Six Years in Camp
   with the Texas Rangers*, Von Boeckmann-Jones Co.,
   Austin.

Roberts, Capt. Daniel Webster.
Rangers and Sovereignty, Wood Printing & Engraving Co., San Antonio, 1914.
Shipman, Mrs. O. L.
Taming the Big Bend, Von Boeckmann-Jones Co., Austin, 1926.
Sullivan, W. J. L.
Twelve Years in the Saddle, Von Boeckmann-Jones Co., Austin, 1909.
Tilghman, Zoe A.
Quanah, The Eagle of the Comanche, Harlow Publishing Corp., Oklahoma City, 1938.
Webb, Walter Prescott.
The Texas Rangers—A Century of Frontier Defense, Houghton, Mifflin Co., New York, 1935.

MAGAZINES

True Detective Mysteries— (Condensed chapters of *Border Boss* were published in this magazine, June-September, 1940, and Copyrighted, 1940, by Macfadden Publications, Inc.)
Everybody's Magazine, September, 1911.
Liberty, May 5, 1928.
Real Detective, September, 1936.
Startling Detective Adventures, September, 1935.
The Cattleman, March, 1937.
True, October, 1938.

NEWSPAPERS

Alice Echo
Alpine Avalanche
Austin Statesman
El Paso Herald
El Paso Times
Marfa New Era
New York Times

San Antonio Express
St. Louis Globe-Democrat
St. Louis Post-Dispatch

UNPUBLISHED

Autobiography of Ira Aten.
Texas Ranger Captains' Reports, 1889-1915.
Texas Adjutant Generals' Reports, 1886-1916.
Correspondence and statements, Old Governors' Palace
    Library, Santa Fé, New Mexico.

INDEX

INDEX